Smart Sourcing

International Best Practice

Andrew Kakabadse

and

Nada Kakabadse

Cranfield School Of Management

palgrave

First published 2002 by
PALGRAVE
Houndmills, Basingstoke, Hampshire RG21 6XS and
175 Fifth Avenue, New York, N. Y. 10010
Companies and representatives throughout the world

PALGRAVE is the new global academic imprint of
St. Martin's Press LLC Scholarly and Reference Division and
Palgrave Publishers Ltd (formerly Macmillan Press Ltd).

ISBN 0–333–96348–2

This book is printed on paper suitable for recycling and
made from fully managed and sustained forest sources.

A catalogue record for this book is available
from the British Library.

Library of Congress Cataloging-in-Publication Data

Kakabadse, Andrew.
    Smart sourcing : international best practice / Andrew Kakabadse and
Nada Kakabadse.
        p.   cm.
    Includes bibliographical references and index.
    ISBN 0–333–96348–2 (cloth)
    1. Contracting out.   2. Privatization.   3. Subcontracting.   4. Government
    purchasing.   5. Industrial procurement.   I. Kakabadse, Nada.   II. Title.

HD2365 .K33 2001
658.7'2—dc21   2001044715

10   9   8   7   6   5   4   3   2   1
11   10   09   08   07   06   05   04   03   02

Printed and bound in Great Britain by
Antony Rowe Ltd, Chippenham, Wiltshire

H50 492 723 8

Please renew/return items by last date shown. Please call the number below:

Renewals and enquiries: 0300 123 4049

Textphone for hearing or
speech impaired users: 0300 123 4041

www.hertsdirect.org/librarycatalogue
L32

Hertfordshire

Smart Sourcing

For the guidance, care and support given in our formative years which has been the platform for our confidence to pursue new challenges, this book is dedicated to our parents, Elfrieda and George Kakabadse and Mila Lisa and Dmitar Korac.

Contents

List of Tables

List of Figures

Preface

What is 'best practice' in outsourcing?
What is happening in outsourcing world-wide?
Are the Americans any better at outsourcing than anyone else?
How does outsourcing enhance shareholder value?
What does it mean to be a 'best run company'?

In this book, we examine the latest thinking and practice in outsourcing and highlight what companies and public service organisations across the world consider to be best practice outsourcing.

The book is intended for the busy manager. The aim is to pinpoint what is happening in terms of outsourcing practice and also to distinguish the essence of top class performance and its relationship with best practice.

Based on the results of an extensive international survey of outsourcing practice, conducted by us, the Cranfield School of Management husband and wife team, Andrew and Nada Kakabadse, comparison is made between the findings of other studies and the results of our research (the Kakabadse survey) in order to highlight the latest trends in outsourcing and thereby pinpoint the nature of outsourcing best practice. Further, interviews are included with senior managers who have given their permission to record their experiences of outsourcing. Finally, case studies of organisations who are experiencing or who, as service providers, are attempting to brand themselves in any interesting fashion, are provided.

Acknowledgements

We wish to thank all those whose support and guidance have made it possible to publish this book.

We thank Dorothy Rogers, Sheena Derby and Alex Britnell for their perseverance and good humour in typing draft after draft.

We also thank Malcolm Stern, surely one of the most accomplished editors we have had the privilege to work with.

Further, we are particularly grateful to Andrew Myers for his invaluable expertise in the extensive and demanding process of data management.

For all those who gave their time to be interviewed, their perspectives substantially contributed to our own thinking. In particular, we thank Don Beattie, President, IPD, David Bell, CEO, Bedfordshire County Council, Graham Brown, National Power, Alun Cole, Partner, Morgan Cole, Tom Drury, CEO, Vertex, Patrick Dunne, CEO, 3iplc, Tonya Hills, CEO, ARFS, Peter Jeffs, head, Central Services, Halifax plc, Justin Jewett, CEO, Nestor Healthcare Group plc, Paul Launders, CEO, Unisource, Jim Leng, CEO, Laporte plc, Michael McGrath, IT Director, Deutsche Bank, Hugh Norton, non-executive director, Lasmo plc, Sir Nigel Rudd, Chairman, Pilkingtons plc, David Scotland, CEO, Allied Domecq, Linda Shaw, Contract Manager, British Airways, Clare Spottiswoode, Chair, Bill Buster and Newco. and former Gas Industry Regulator, Andrew Teare, portfolio non-executive director, Vanni Treeves, Chairman, Channel Four Television, BBA Group plc, London Business School, Eamus Halpin, CEO, iRevolution Ltd, David Mills, Vice President, FutureLink, Europe Ltd, Ian Symon, CEO, Pragmatas, Chris Murphy, Operations Director, Pragmatas and Martin Walker, Chair, Software and as a Service Forum.

1
Introduction

Numerous writers conclude that the greatest benefit an enterprise can derive from outsourcing is cost reduction. They argue that pursuing outsourcing for the purposes of economies of scale produces not only a cost advantage but also increased internal efficiencies. Others argue that outsourcing can strategically change an organisation, assisting management to analyse the extent to which the firm is differentiated from its competitors and thus emerge with a clear value proposition for the enterprise. As a result, resources are repositioned to be more focused on achieving particular goals and targets.

Outsourcing involves contracting with a third party to provide goods and services to the host organisation that would have been available in-house. The most common motive for sourcing out the responsibility for managing particular resources to other parties is that it has become unprofitable for the host organisation to maintain them within the corporate framework. Most markets in which enterprises operate are held to be maturing. Thus differentiating the enterprise from the competition is becoming ever necessary as the consumers of the company's goods and services and the owners (shareholders) of the enterprise will switch their attention and loyalties elsewhere, if, in their eyes, value for money is not delivered. It is the appropriate positioning (sourcing) of resources that provides the enterprise the leverage it needs to meet consumer demands in terms of quality and/or price and to satisfy shareholder requirements for continued profitability and growth.

Its current popularity masks the fact that outsourcing, originally called the contracting out of organisational activities, is not a new phenomenon. For example, the Romans contracted out tax collection. In eighteenth and nineteenth century, England public services were serviced by the private sector in the form of street lighting, prison management, road maintenance, the collection of taxes and other public revenues and even refuse collection, under contract to local authorities. During the same period, similar arrangements existed in America and Australia, whereby private operations provided mail delivery and in France the construction and management of the railway network and other distribution facilities was contracted out to commercial companies through competitive tendering. As the industrial revolution proceeded throughout the western world, contractual relationships of varying forms between government and the private sector dominated the organisation of production and distribution.

Matters changed with the onset of the twentieth century. Volume based production encouraged the large, vertically integrated enterprise, as opposed to the myriad of smaller organisations providing contractually based services on behalf of government. A comparable pattern of vertical integration was adopted by the state on behalf of the public bureaucracy machinery of government. Such developments reversed the trend towards contracting out.

Ironically, the very same factors that led to a retreat from contracting out have fostered its resurgence over the past 15 years. It is no longer cost effective to maintain specialist services in-house, as greater professional and economic benefit is gained by releasing such resources into the market place to fend for themselves. On this basis, external providers are now offered the opportunity to deliver services on a scale that many single organisations would find it difficult to match. Accompanying such changes of organisational form has been a change of mindset from management to leadership. The perception that relative power within organisations is symbolised by size of budget and the number of employees within a manager's domain, has been replaced by concern with concepts such as profitability and value enhancement. Managers are more interested in running lean organisations than large empires. Managing internal organisational processes is giving way to achieving targets and demonstrating value.

Why smart sourcing?

The impact of outsourcing on the host organisation varies from one enterprise to the next, ranging from identifying and applying tactical solutions to practical problems at one end, such as contracting out routine ancillary services, to clarifying the strategic direction that needs to be pursued by the organisation, at the other. To integrate a variety of initiatives, from the tactical to the strategic, and in ways that meet the needs of the host enterprise, being contextually sensitive and yet economically valid requires being 'smart'.

The word 'smart', in the sense of weighing up circumstances and being both efficient in the use of resources and effective in delivering the desired outcomes, has been applied in a number of ways. 'Working smarter', meaning being more productive through better use of time by rethinking what one does, is a commonly heard phrase. 'Smart technology' supported by 'smart software', represents accuracy and speed in terms of economically accessing data, or of forecasting by integrating different information sources. 'Smart performance' arises when synergy between the various parts of the organisation is achieved through enlightened management. 'Smart strategies' integrate the mission and vision of the organisation with operational plans to generate unique knowledge which the company can leverage. Further, the term 'smart' has been adopted at an organisational level where, through good management, entire processes and teams use knowledge as their primary asset. It has even been applied to government, whereby politicians and senior civil servants focus on their strategic role in society, through designing public institutions and developing the managerial capabilities of public servants to meet the needs of the population at large.

When applied to outsourcing, 'smart' denotes having considered how to gain advantage through the repositioning of enterprise resources and then effectively managing one or a number of supplier relationships. Smart sourcing focuses as much on the transformational capabilities of identifying ways forward and being effective at the motivation of and communication with people, as on the transactional skills of managing the detailed aspects of business and the routine application of technology.

General Manager, Business Consultancy, Kakabadse Survey Participant

A smart company anticipates the challenges associated with the outsourcing of its activities and takes an active approach to minimise the discomfort of its employees. My experience shows that it is impossible to avoid some dip in employee morale when a company makes an outsourcing announcement, but it is possible to avoid its long term effects. HR arrangements can make or break an outsourcing initiative.

Thus successful private and public sector enterprises are ones that have smartly sourced their enterprises in ways which secure economies of scale and yet also provide improvements in quality of service, whilst working in partnership with suppliers in different competitive networks to achieve optimum results. Hence, smart sourcing involves managing an array of sourcing contracts and arrangements that helps the enterprise to concentrate on achieving its strategic and operational goals.

The book

Smart sourcing requires both the transformational capabilities for positioning the organisation to attain competitive advantage and the transactional skills for managing outsourcing arrangements. With this as their central theme, the following chapters examine current and predicted future trends in outsourcing, against which are presented the results of the Kakabadse survey. Throughout the book, emphasis is placed on how to prepare an organisation to manage a variety of contractual relationships so as to increase its effectiveness.

Chapter 2 outlines current trends in outsourcing thinking and practice. It looks at the variety of reasons for outsourcing, the nature of sourcing arrangements and the outcomes of outsourcing in terms of value to the host organisation and of customer satisfaction. Throughout Chapter 2, comparison is made between trends described by other writers and the trends emerging from the Kakabadse survey. The Kakabadse survey also compares outsourcing trends and practices in the United States of America, United Kingdom and Europe and identifies significant differences.

Chapter 3 examines outsourcing best practice. From a sample of over 747 private and public sector organisations, 69 stand out in terms of distinguished outsourcing performance. The two key factors that differentiate the 69 companies from the others are the quality of top team leadership and the emphasis on customer care and customer satisfaction. High-performing and average-performing companies are compared according to their reasons for outsourcing, the various types of outsourcing contracts entered into with suppliers, the arrangements made for employees affected by outsourcing, the value gained from outsourcing and the quality of relationship that has evolved between service purchasers and their suppliers. The Kakabadse survey also identifies the particular capabilities and skills required for achieving outsourcing best practice. Again high-performing and average-performing companies are compared in terms of levels of preparedness to apply the particular best practice capabilities. The key conclusion to emerge from Chapter 3 is that high quality top team leadership is fundamental to effective outsourcing. Once top management recognise what is required to change and how to drive through change, outsourcing in high-performing organisations becomes a lever for repositioning the enterprise to promote higher quality, value for money services.

Chapter 4 examines what the senior managers who participated in the Kakabadse survey consider the future to be for outsourcing practice.

The emerging view is that current trends are likely to continue into the foreseeable future. The only telling difference between current practice and probable future trends is that greater emphasis is likely to be given to managing horizontal, partner-like relationships between the host organisation and suppliers. The 'keiretsu', partner-like, nature of future outsourcing is predicted to require organisations to be better prepared to enter into outsourcing initiatives, in effect for organisations to become far more 'outsource ready'. Attention is given to examining what is required to become outsource ready. In so doing, it is identified how the best run companies are likely to position themselves to manage future outsourcing programmes.

Chapter 5 explores outsourcing in the public services. The history of public service organisations, post-Second World War, paints a picture of fundamental change, from the administration of vertically integrated, large public bureaucracies, concerned with the delivery of services for the public good, providing longevity of employment for public servants, to slimmed down organisations focused on 'value for money' delivery, balancing the demands for increased level of service with the constraint of diminishing resources. To give a better appreciation of the capability for pursuing outsourcing contracts, comparison is made between public service organisations, professional services enterprises and companies from the manufacturing, engineering and construction sectors. The emerging trend is that managing contractual relationships between the host organisation and its suppliers is a particular strength of public servant managers. However, public servants express the greatest degree of dissatisfaction with outsourcing, indicating that little value is realised from sourcing out organisational processes and activities. Also public service organisations experience the poorest quality of relationship between themselves and their suppliers. The reason for such dissatisfaction is that public service managers view changes to the infrastructure of the organisation as driven by political motivations. The chapter concludes that until political interests are better aligned with the managerial interests of running public service organisations, any attempt to reposition resources is likely to be met with hostility.

Chapter 6 explores the newest of entrants into the outsourcing arena, the application service providers (ASPs). The information technology (IT) outsourcing market is moving fast, having now reached a point of providing rental services for the meeting of information systems requirements, thus freeing the end user from having to outlay substantial capital costs. The growth of this market and its impact on SMEs (small to medium sized enterprises) and larger corporate organisations is discussed.

As this market is less than four years old, the variety of views available in the literature is scant. However, what is clear is the growth market potential of ASPs and the advantages and disadvantages that they bring with them. The Cranfield survey highlights that customer satisfaction with ASPs is greater than expected and equally informs as to the emerging profile of ASPs and ASP users. The chapter concludes by providing two case studies of ASPs, an HR sourcing start-up, Pragmatas, searching for its first client and how a number of ASPs have clustered around a major vendor, Microsoft, in order to leverage off the Microsoft brand, enhance their access to channels to market, upgrade the quality of their applications through interaction with each other, and gain advantage through improved economies of scale. The need to migrate around a major vendor is understandable, as current evidence highlights that 80 per cent or so of present ASPs will fold over the next two years.

Each chapter ends with a section entitled 'References and further reading'. This contains details of other works referred to in the chapter and lists additional reading which may be of interest to the reader. Preference is given to the most recently published material.

The survey

The Kakabadse survey was undertaken in two stages; initial interviews to ascertain key issues and trends in outsourcing, followed by a more

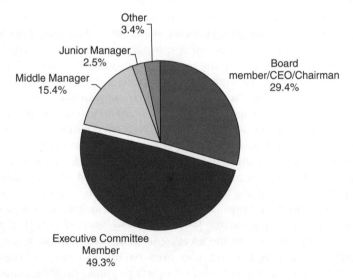

Figure 1.1   Level in the organisation.

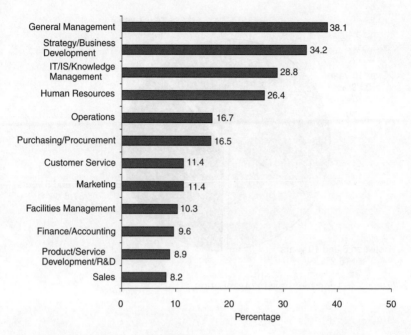

Figure 1.2 Functional responsibilities.
Note: Many respondents ticked more than one option highlighting the duality or great complexity of their role.

comprehensive, empirically based survey of UK, European and North American organisations which was completed by June 2001. As stated, 747 respondents took part. The key theme to emerge is that outsourcing best practice depends on the degree to which a coherent view exists at top team level concerning the value to be gained from outsourcing. Such clarity of view and consistency of 'push' down the organisation is a prerequisite for a consistent approach to managing outsourced relationships. The survey identifies the capabilities required for effective outsourcing. A strong outsourcing capability in the host organisation is found to be a necessary element for achieving desired outcomes.

Over 78 per cent of the respondents in the survey are senior managers who are either Board members (either executive or non-executive directors) and, or, members of the Executive Committee (principally executive directors (Figure 1.1). The greater proportion occupy a general management, or strategy/business development role, which for many is part of a broader functional role (Figure 1.2). As far as organisational tenure is concerned, 54 per cent of the respondents indicate that they

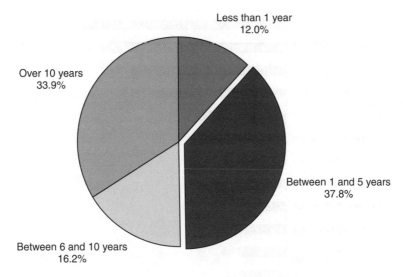

Figure 1.3 Length of time in organisation.

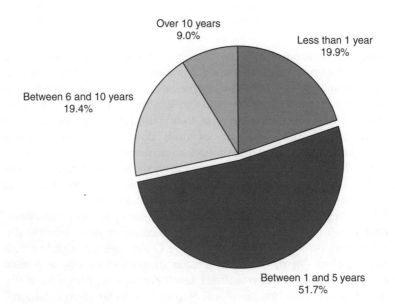

Figure 1.4 Length of time in role.

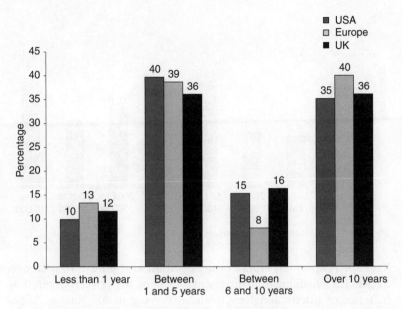

Figure 1.5 Organisation tenure: international comparison.

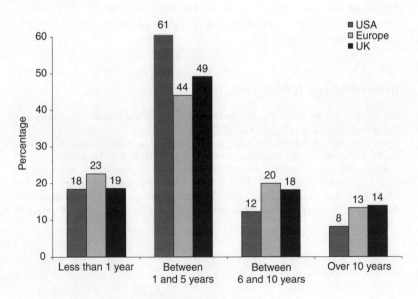

Figure 1.6 Role tenure: international comparison.

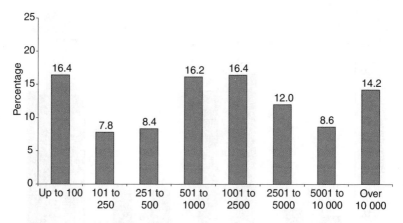

Figure 1.7   Total number of employees.

have spent up to ten years in the organisation (Figure 1.3), with over 51 per cent remaining in their present role for up to five years (Figure 1.4). In terms of international comparison, varying trends emerge. Senior managers in US companies emphasise more limited organisational tenure (5 years) and the Europeans for a ten-year tenure (Figure 1.5). Further, the greater number of managers of US companies remain in their role for up to five years (Figure 1.6). Concerning the size of organisation, over 51 per cent of the respondents are employed in enterprises of over 1000 employees (Figure 1.7).

References and further reading

For further information on the history of outsourcing (contracting out), see Kakabadse and Kakabadse (2000a; 2000b).

For developments in outsourcing in the latter half of the twentieth century, read Domberger (1998), Venkatraman (1997), and Finlay and King (1999).

For insights as to how the word 'smart' has been applied in the management and organisational literature, read Bowen (1984) for working smarter, Tissen et al. (2000) for smart organisations, Kliksberg (2000) for smart government and Earl (1996), Vineeta (1994) and Morrell (1998) for the application of smart to outsourcing.

2
Emerging Trends

Case study: outsourcing leisure

Interview: Senior Manager, large leisure Group.
Interviewee wished to remain anonymous.

Q. What are your prime motives for outsourcing?

A. The primary driver, I think, is to achieve cost benefits. We can cut down our costs, whether that is operational costs or whether it's the total cost of technology, by outsourcing. An additional valid reason for outsourcing is to use somebody else's experience and for a price you can give somebody else your problem.

Q. What benefits have been achieved through outsourcing?

A. Substantial. We have done some fairly large outsource projects. Some have worked better than others.

Q. The function/processes being outsourced, are they core, enabling supportive or what?

A. Pretty much everything. We have outsourced our legacy systems ...We have outsourced Web design...We have outsourced other small businesses... We have outsourced all our hardware management. None of our companies run their own hardware maintenance.

Box   *Continued*

Q.   What about the skills for managing outsourced contracts?

A.   That's the challenge. Finding the people with the right skills to manage outsource contracts is becoming increasingly important. A lot of people have tried to sell us an outsourcing project on the grounds that they take that management responsibility... but the cost equation never actually says that for every 50 people on the outsource side, we are going to need a full time manager, and a senior level manager at that. I spent about a year and a half working on a major telecoms outsource contract, where we wanted to outsource all our telecoms, voice data, video and other things, globally. We got into difficult negotiations with our provider. We were looking for £20 million savings per year for five years for that size of contract. The thing really fell apart because we couldn't convince ourselves that we could manage the contract and the provider could offer the quality in a way we could actually measure.

Q.   What about quality of relationship with suppliers?

A.   Outsourcers will talk about partnerships. They want to talk about partnerships because that is nice and fuzzy and warm and psychologically appealing. The reality is that, at the end of the day, it's a commercial contract.

B.   Do the terms 'value' and 'value added' have any meaning or significance at the top of your organisation?

A.   No to meaning, yes to significance. Because of the different lines of business that we are in, conflicting viewpoints exist at senior levels concerning the meaning of 'value'. Also we are trying to balance short-term and long-term considerations, which is not easy. The problem is that in our company the various businesses have their own business drivers. On top of that, the overall decider is that the strategic direction for the Group is survival.

Q.   Are outsourcing decisions taken at Board level?

A.   Yes, as a lot of our outsourcing projects are simply big.

Q.   What do you look for in your outsourcing providers?

A.   If you are going to outsource the function as opposed to the mechanism, you require somebody who understands the function.

> We've outsourced our pensions operation, not with the EDS's or IBM's, but to a specialist financial institution who provides the complete package. We want the specialist broker, not so much the large houses who write the computer system. It's going to be functional rather than technology outsourcers who will probably do better in the future.

The interview is wide ranging, covering issues such as size of outsourcing contracts, where sourcing decisions are made, sourcing reasons, the processes/functions being outsourced, sourcing arrangements and the outcomes of outsourcing. This senior manager takes a positive view of outsourcing. He also indicates he has little choice but to outsource, as the need to reduce costs is critical to the future survival of the enterprise. The senior manager highlights an additional issue, that of the all embracing impact of outsourcing on the organisation. The message is that outsourcing has now become a fundamental, strategic consideration for the company.

An overview of recent outsourcing deals supports this manager's perspective. Table 2.1 shows the size of a number of outsourcing activities conducted across a variety of sectors with varying numbers of suppliers involved, which in some cases are single suppliers and in others take the form of partnership or consortium arrangements. The outsourcing contracts listed are substantial, ranging from US$220 million to US$3 billion. Inevitably, contracts of such a size have a fundamental impact on the whole organisation.

In keeping with the themes to have emerged from the interview with the service manager of the leisure group company, the range of topics covered in this chapter is wide. We discuss trends in outsourcing practice and the impact of outsourcing on organisations over the last two decades. Through case examples and by comparing the outsourcing strategies adopted by US, UK and European companies, we demonstrate the different approaches to outsourcing that exist. We also look at some of the changes taking place in the outsourcing market and assess the impact of such changes on the more 'established' service providers. Throughout, we compare the trends identified in the academic and business literature and the results of the Kakabadse international survey.

The Kakabadse survey sets out to capture the latest trends and practices in outsourcing and their impact on service purchasers, service providers and other stakeholders.

Table 2.1 Recent European outsourcing deals (upto June 2001)

Service provider(s)	Client	Sector	Value $US
IBM	Cable and Wireless	Telecom	3 bn
TranSystems consortium; EDS; Cubic Crop, ICL and WS Atkins	London Transport	Transport	1.6 bn
Siemens	National Savings	Banking	1.5 bn
EDS	Banka di Roma	Banking	1.5 bn
Sema Group	Department of Social Services	Local Government (UK)	500 m
ICL	Department of Trade and Industry	Government (UK)	330 m
FI Group	First Banking System, Bank of Scotland	Banking	246 m
IBM	IS Consortium Caricentro	Banking	235 m
Siemens	Passport Agency	Government (UK)	220 m
Unisys	Abbey Life (Lloyds TSB Group)	Insurance	300 m
IBM	BP	Petroleum	200 m
Lanarkshire-based Stiell Group	Bank of Scotland	Bank	190 m
IBM	NTL	Cable	2 bn
IBM Global services	Fiat	Car manufacturing	7 bn

Source: Compiled from *Dataquest* (1999), Foremski (2000), *Agence France Presse* (2000), Bain (2000), Heikkila (2001), Mathieson (2001), M2 Communications Ltd (2001), McCure (2001).

The rest of this chapter analyses the trends and the survey results in the following areas:

- the reasons for outsourcing – sourcing reasons;
- the activities, processes and functions being outsourced, – sourcing what;
- the nature of the outsourcing arrangements being adopted – sourcing how;
- the profile of the most-to-least preferred suppliers – sourcing with whom;
- the arrangements entered into for employees affected by outsourcing;
- the impact of outsourcing on the host organisation;
- the degree of satisfaction with outsourcing.

Sourcing reasons

The senior manager interviewed in the leisure case study clearly identifies cost as the prime reason for outsourcing, and as he states 'the motivation is survival!' What also emerges from the interview is that the senior managers in his organisation do not share an agreed view concerning what is a core competence that should be kept in-house and what is non-core and should be outsourced. In fact, the interviewee has raised a prime consideration in outsourcing, the strong interrelationship between the reason(s) for outsourcing and determining what needs to be outsourced.

Emerging trends

Outsourcing for the purposes of achieving economies of scale, namely cost advantage, has been and continues to be a prominent reason for outsourcing. The Boston Consulting Group examined the outsourcing practices of more than 100 organisations and concluded that most western companies outsource primarily to save on overheads through short-term cost savings. This finding has been echoed by other studies, which show that, until the 1990s, the main reason for IT outsourcing was cost-effective access to specialised computing and system development skills and special external functional capabilities. The conclusion was: do not invest heavily in building in-house IT skills. The trade off was between lower production costs – assuming the supplier possesses lower cost technology – and higher monitoring costs.

Throughout the 1990s global competition compelled large companies to apply greater discipline over costs and over product to market time cycles, resulting in a smaller product and services portfolio and a loosening of the vertical links in the production process. As a result, corporations have divested what they regard as elements peripheral to their business so as to focus upon their 'core' business. Reliance on the vertically driven organisation has been reduced. In turn, greater emphasis has been given to horizontal relationships so as to improve quality, whilst paying attention to cost effectiveness. For example, in 1999 Unilever, the Anglo-Dutch group, with a portfolio of 1600 food, toiletries and household products, announced that, to enhance sales growth and profitability, it would focus on a smaller number of 'power brands' (core products) which would have greater worldwide reach. The aim is to reduce costs and exploit new channels of distribution, such as the internet. The search for greater efficiency, leading to increased specialisation, coupled with attempting to achieve other value adding objectives, added a new dimension to outsourcing, that of attempting to manage multiple, but, at times, ill fitting sourcing strategies. Such managerial gymnastics have masked a more fundamental issue, that of determining what is core to the host organisation so that those processes and activities that are considered peripheral can be passed over to an external service provider.

Determining what is core and non-core to the organisation, whilst attempting to attain multiple outcomes through outsourcing, has been a focal point of debate. Some regard core activities as representative of core competences, in that those areas in which the firm is continuously engaged are fundamental to the survival of the enterprise. On this basis, peripheral activities can be outsourced. However, certain writers consider that what is core and what is peripheral is an academic debate, as outsourcing decisions should be driven by the nature of sourcing contracts, the contractual and informal relationships between the purchaser and supplier, the use of market opportunities to determine greater competitive advantage and the successful management of contracts, which, in turn, lead to the development of a new cluster of core competences. The view proposed is that administering outsourced relationships becomes itself a core competence. The reason is that an inability to manage outsourced relationships could mean that competitive advantage is not gained as the poorly developed service purchaser/service provider relationship inhibits fully leveraging the competences available from the service provider.

Still others advocate concentrating solely on competitive advantage, arguing that core competences are those activities that offer long-term competitive advantage and thus should be kept in-house. They contend that activities that used to be integral to the organisation, but for which the firm has no strategic need, can be outsourced. Thus was coined the term 'strategic outsourcing', emphasising what competences are fundamental to the firm and necessary to achieve its strategic goals. Nike, for example, outsourced shoe production and manufactures only the key elements of its 'Nike Air' system on the basis that Nike creates maximum value by concentrating on what is unique to them, namely, research and development and post-production activities. Other Nike activities such as distribution, sales and marketing (with the exception of advertising) have been outsourced. In similar vein, Argyle Diamonds, a major diamond producer, has outsourced all aspects of its operations (earth-moving operations, housing and services for workers, distribution) to best-in-class suppliers. However, what has been kept in-house is the separation and the sorting of diamonds, which is considered core to the organisation. A further example are Apple Computers, who outsource 70 per cent of their manufacturing as well as additional activities such as design, and even aspects of marketing, in order to focus on the production of items such as Apple DOS (disk operating system) and the supporting macro software, which give Apple products their unique look and feel.

According to a third view of the economies of scale vs. the strategic sourcing argument, outsourcing is now all embracing and not concentrated on one activity or function. A recent study by Pricewaterhouse-Coopers established that outsourcing has moved markedly from more efficiently attending to a single function to reconfiguring a whole process to realise greater value across the enterprise. The current trend is from outsourcing parts, facilities and components towards outsourcing intellectual systems such as customer response handling, procurement and management. DaimlerChrysler, for example, outsourced the management of its supplier relationship portfolio to Andersen Consulting, for the production of the 'smart car' in France.

The Kakabadse survey

Three distinct clusters of reasons for undertaking outsourcing are identified (Figure 2.1). First, aiming to achieve best practice across the enterprise and to also enhance the cost discipline and control competences of the organisation score closely and form the first cluster. Additionally, attempting to improve service quality whilst equally focusing on better leveraging the core competences of the organisation emerge as the second cluster of reasons for undertaking outsourcing. Further, gaining access to new technology and skills that were not available in the organisation, reducing headcount, enhancing the organisation's capability to develop new products and services and reduce capital costs, are identified as the third cluster of reasons for outsourcing. In effect, the operational skills of aiming to achieve best practice and improving the cost discipline skills of managers in the organisation are pursued in conjunction with determining and leveraging what is core to the organisation across the enterprise. The Kakabadse survey results emphasise that through outsourcing, as much attention is given to reducing costs as to strategically focusing the organisation to gain greater competitive advantage.

International comparison between US, UK and European companies reveals a similar pattern (Figure 2.2). However, European and US companies give different reasons for outsourcing. European companies identify cost discipline and control as their main motives, whereas aiming to achieve best practice is a key driver for US enterprises. The more developmental orientation displayed by US companies for pursuing outsourcing is reinforced, as senior US managers rate improving service quality,

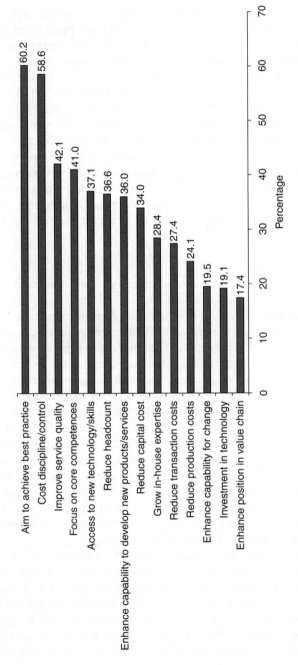

Figure 2.1 Sourcing reasons.
Note: Respondents selected multiple options.

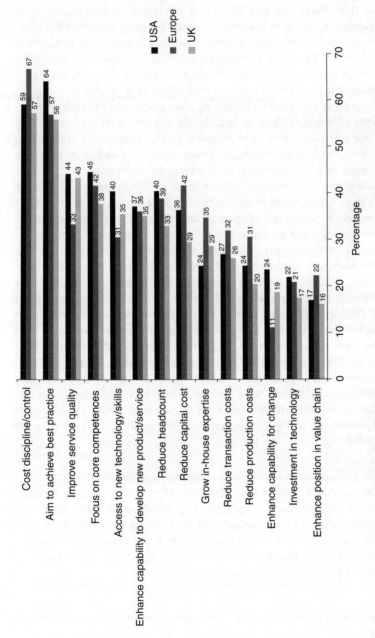

Figure 2.2 Sourcing reasons: international comparison.
Note: Respondents selected multiple options.

focusing on core competences and accessing new technology and skills higher than European and UK senior managers. Senior managers of European companies, in particular, display a greater proclivity for reducing costs, particularly capital costs, transaction costs and production costs. Further, European companies report giving greater attention to growing in-house expertise to manage a number of different processes, activities and functions. European companies give greater attention to enhancing the company's position in the value chain through outsourcing, than US and UK companies. European companies emphasise that they use outsourcing to help realise a greater number of contrasting objectives, ranging from enhanced cost disciplines and cost reduction to growing in-house expertise, than US and UK companies.

The survey results emphasise that for many companies, outsourcing is not undertaken solely to satisfy the need for cost disciplines. The US companies, in particular, adopt a more strategically oriented approach to outsourcing through concurrently aiming to achieve best practice, improving service quality, focusing on the core competences of the organisation, attempting to apply new technology more effectively throughout the organisation's processes and systems, while all the time maintaining a discipline on costs. Examples of improvements in product and service quality whilst applying cost effective measures can be seen in the US auto industry, where, for example, Chrysler estimated that supplier cost reduction efforts ('SCORE') would add $235 million to its profits for the fiscal year 1997 and eventually generate over $1.2 billion in savings. Similarly, General Motors insist that its 30 000 worldwide parts suppliers must hold warranty costs below predetermined levels and through such discipline attempt to eliminate waste through the entire supply chain, all while improvements in the quality of production are continued.

We did a major project over about an 18-month period to fundamentally change the way the Group operated and initially to move towards a shared service model, but very clearly in the back of our minds was the prospect of outsourcing significant chunks of that work once we'd got it packaged in an outsourceable way – Don Beattie, President CIPD; Former Personnel Director, BOC

Irrespective of whether economy of scale or integrated or even loosely coupled clusters of outsourcing strategies are being pursued, the survey findings support the views of Don Beattie and the PricewaterhouseCoopers conclusion of the 'all embracing impact' of outsourcing on the host organisation. The trends presented on Figure 2.3 show that the processes, activities and functions that are outsourced are seen as critical to the future survival of the enterprise. Even those outsourced activities that are viewed as non-critical to the future functioning of the organisation, are reported as supporting the organisational strategies already being pursued. Despite the fact that most of what is outsourced is considered as holding commodity status, the senior managers in the survey recognise an alignment between those activities outsourced and the strategies being pursued by the organisation.

In contrast to the trends identified by other writers and researchers, the survey also shows that a substantial proportion of outsourced activities are supported by mature technology, emphasising the commodity status of the activities and processes outsourced.

Differentiating the enterprise against the competition by using leading edge technology and knowledge management capabilities is low on the list of outsourcing priorities.

International comparison of the impact of outsourcing on the host organisation indicates that UK senior managers view outsourced activities and processes as supporting the core strategy being pursued by the organisation and critical to the functioning of the enterprise (Figure 2.4). US senior managers are more likely to regard outsourced activities as being of commodity status but as having a powerful impact on how the rest of the organisation operates. Although the use of leading edge technology by US, UK and European companies falls lower on their list of priorities, US companies report a greater preference for the adoption of latest technology through outsourcing in order to provide competitive advantage for the enterprise.

The emerging trends from both the literature and the Kakabadse survey support the 'variety of reasons for outsourcing' viewpoint. Further, the Kakabadse survey, the perspective of Don Beattie and the Pricewaterhouse-Coopers study all indicate that, irrespective of whether one or more functions are under scrutiny at any time, the process of outsourcing and the results of outsourcing deeply affect how the organisation functions. The far-reaching impact of outsourcing on the host organisation is recognised by senior management and reflected in the fact that the decisions to outsource are largely made at senior management levels (Figure 2.5). The Kakabadse survey results indicate that over 57 per cent of sourcing decisions are made at top manager level, relatively evenly split between those made at board level (involving executive and non-executive directors)

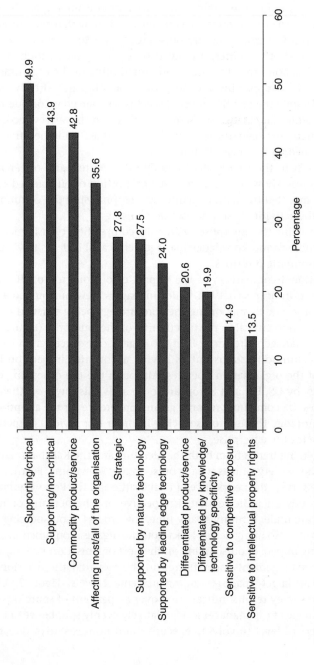

Figure 2.3 Status of activities/processes outsourced.
Note: Respondents selected multiple options.

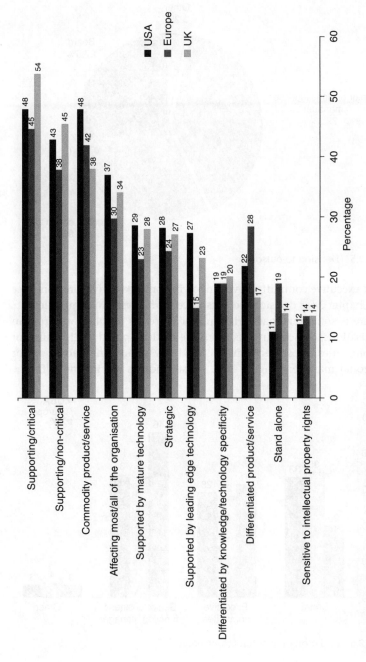

Figure 2.4 Status of outsourced activity: international comparison.
Note: Respondents selected multiple options.

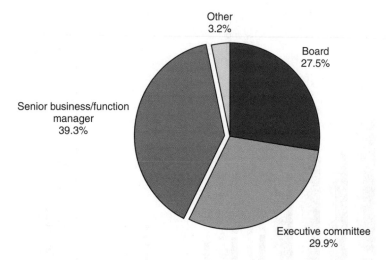

Figure 2.5   Decision to outsource.

and at executive committee level (involving only executive directors – see also Chapter 3 for decisions to outsource in the best run companies).

There is some regional variation. For a greater number of European organisations, outsourcing decisions are made at board level, whilst for US companies, most decisions are made by senior line and/or senior functional managers (Figure 2.6). These findings are in line with the

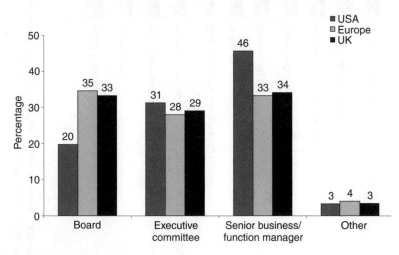

Figure 2.6   Initiation of decision to outsource.

results of other studies, namely that the sourcing debate is making its way up the organisation to CIO (Chief Information Officer), CFO (Chief Finance Officer) or CEO (Chief Executive Officer) levels. As argued at the start of this chapter in the Outsourcing Leisure case study, a prelude to the making of sourcing decisions is the reaching of consensus at senior levels concerning the value to be gained from undertaking outsourcing. The survey results show that is more important for the senior management of UK and European companies to emerge with a cohesive view concerning the value outsourcing can provide, as outsourcing comes to take on a substantially greater strategic significance for them. The more mature market position of North America and the greater experience of US management in tackling outsourcing challenges indicates that locating and realising value in the organisation is a more familiar activity for senior US line managers. Thus for US companies, outsourcing is more of an operational tool, as the key strategic issues are likely to have been already clarified and a way forward agreed and committed to by senior management (see Chapter 3 on the importance of cohesive top teams in ensuring outsourcing success).

Sourcing what?

As shown by the Kakabadse survey and other studies and reports, there can be many different reasons for deciding to outsource. Bearing in mind the importance attached to outsourcing, the question arises what needs to be outsourced in order to realise the potential advantages. The area that has received most attention in the outsourcing literature has been IT.

Emerging trends

Global competition, downsizing, the move to flatter organisations, the search for greater flexibility, rapid changes in technology and the emphasis on core competences, are cited as causes of the upsurge in IT outsourcing. In the IT industry, data storage capability has dramatically increased in quality and at the same time has become significantly cheaper, to the extent that data storage services are being charged on a cost-per-megabyte-per-month basis, in a similar way that clients pay for utilities like electricity and water. As such, IT has acquired more of a 'commodity' status. Consequently, companies in their pursuit of gaining competitive advantage have been increasing their reliance on external suppliers of information services. Thus, the outsourcing of IT has grown at a phenomenal rate over the past decade in North America, the

United Kingdom and Australia. Western Europe, South America and parts of South East Asia, including Japan, are now following suit, having previously resisted the trend.

The IT market analysts, the Gartner Group, have projected a 16.3 per cent growth rate, world-wide, between 1997 and 2002, estimating a $120 billion IT outsourcing market by 2002. The US market is projected to account for $51 billion of this amount. In similar vein, research conducted at the International Data Corporation (IDC) forecasts a global IT market of more than $151 billion by 2003. The study also concludes that processing services, which include payroll, claims and credit card processing are, and will continue to be, the most popular outsourced activities.

Furthermore, e-commerce is redefining the trading world in terms of 'make, buy, process, sell' decisions. Setting up a web site for online sales can be expensive and requires in-house expertise in server management, security and a myriad of related technical functions. Such expertise is in short supply. Small and medium sized companies are increasingly turning to external service providers to host their web sites. These external suppliers provide an e-commerce infrastructure, such as credit card processing, virtual shopping carts and help in promoting web sites. Hewlett-Packard, for example, launched an outsourcing service, HP Emporium, aimed at companies taking their first hesitant steps in e-commerce. HP Emporium offers a complete package, comprising web site hosting and services, covering the whole of the e-commerce life cycle, including merchandising, security, financial transactions and logistics. In Europe, various companies are pursuing a similar route. For example, British Telecom plan to offer a special version of SAP's R3 accounting and payroll modules. Further, J.D. Edwards with Catalyst Solutions and Cable and Wireless are seeking to provide comparable services to companies in the £50 million-a-year turnover bracket. In effect, many internet service providers (ISPs) have started offering design services and are keen to extend into outsourcing in order to reduce their dependence on basic internet access. Forester Research Inc. predicts that the market for server hosting will grow to more than $10.5 billion, the market for complex internet hosting will grow to $8 billion by 2002, whilst applications in the rental market will grow from virtually nothing, 18 months ago, to $6 billion by late 2001.

Even software suppliers have adopted outsourcing arrangements through spin off activities and are forming ASP organisations to supply and manage applications remotely, charging a flat fee per user. Oracle of the United States of America, SAP of Germany and Baan of The Netherlands, as well as Telecomputing of Oslo, are offering ASP services as a mechanism to deliver their, often complex, software to the small and medium enterprise market.

Increasingly, outsourcing suppliers are looking beyond running IT systems to business process management (BPM) through which they also take over functions such as billing, cheque processing and accounting. Many of these contracts incorporate an element of shared risk, in which the supplier's remuneration depends on the increase in profit at the client company end or through the success of a joint venture enterprise. For example, Andersen Consulting and Pacific Dunlop have set up a 50/50 joint venture to provide for the full range of business support and IT functions across multi-client service locations (MSLs). The relationship with Pacific Dunlop will be Andersen Consulting's 20th international MSL.

According to the Gartner Group, BPM is now the fastest-growing element of the outsourcing market, rising from $6.1 billion in 1997 to an expected $14.7 billion by 2002. Such a dramatic market rise has led to further redefinition of the market by providers who are setting up shared service centres (SSC). Shared service centres provide a range of IT services across particular sectors. The oil industry accounting centre in Aberdeen is just one example. The centre was originally set up in 1991 by Andersen Consulting to service BP Amoco and now serves ten clients, all oil companies. A similar venture was established near Wilmington in the US State of Delaware to offer IT solutions for six large chemical companies, including the core client, DuPont. By adopting common technology systems and infrastructure, individual company costs can be reduced by 50 per cent. Furthermore, through using the same processes and working at the same open-plan site, the integrity of information is better safeguarded.

The Kakabadse survey

> Catering, we outsourced all our airline catering three years ago... Our key skills as an airline were not in food production. Therefore as a catering business, we could not sustain a cost effective operation... we outsourced all our property maintenance eight years ago for two main reasons. An obvious one was to reduce our operating spend and secondly was looking to reduce headcount in areas which were not deemed core business – Linda Shaw, General Manager, British Airways

In keeping with the attention given to IT outsourcing in the literature, the Kakabadse survey indicates that basic services, IT and human resources (HR) activities and related processes are the most commonly outsourced functions (Figure 2.7). In support of these findings, Linda Shaw identifies basic services, such as catering and property maintenance, as areas for outsourcing. The IT-based services emerge as second on the list of processes and functions being outsourced confirming what other studies have found. In contrast to the trends identified in other studies, the outsourcing of e-commerce related activities and call centres are rated as being of less importance, in fact, below facilities management. Similar trends emerge from an international comparison (Figure 2.8). The US companies attend more to outsourcing basic services (ranging from canteen facilities to office services), whereas UK companies marginally give greater attention to IT outsourcing. In contrast, European companies focus more on HR and manufacturing outsourcing. Lower in the rankings, but considered as being of substantial importance to US and UK companies, is technology based outsourcing, particularly in telecommunication services and e-commerce related activities. Also US companies give greater attention to facilities management outsourcing than UK or European companies.

Sourcing how?

With so many reasons for, and needs to be served by, outsourcing, what form of contractual and structural relationships have been entered into by service purchasers and service providers to achieve their outsourcing objectives?

Emerging trends

An examination of the arrangements between service purchasers/service providers reveals a variety of forms, from, at one end, short term contracts designated to encourage flexibility, to, at the other, full ownership of, and/or merger between, service purchasers and service providers. Between these extremes lie alternative arrangements involving partial ownership, joint developments, retainers and other long-term contracts, single contracts, relationships with preferred and trusted suppliers, multiple vendor contracts, joint ventures, individual and joint venture spin-offs, consortia and shared service consortia.

The emergence of partnership or alliance arrangements as alternatives to the more popular transaction based contracts (usually shorter, single contract, with a preferred, trusted supplier), has been interpreted as offering a closer level of interaction between client and provider. Although partnership arrangements vary considerably, from flexibly defined formal contracts to loose strategic initiatives, most involve shared

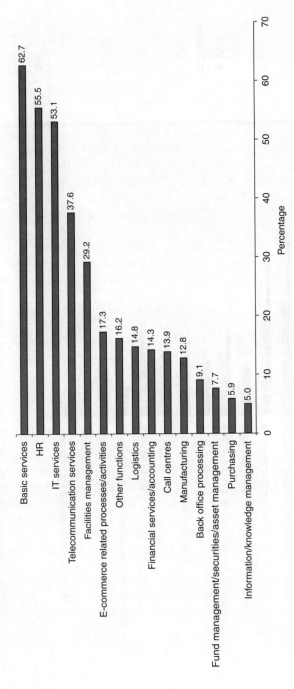

Figure 2.7 Business processes/functions outsourced.
Note: Respondents selected multiple options.

30

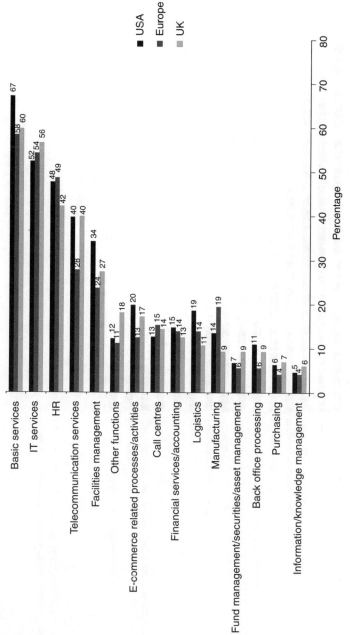

Figure 2.8 Business processes/functions outsourced: international comparison.
Note: Respondents selected multiple options.

risk and benefit. The emerging assumption in the literature is that a single vendor does not possess world-class capabilities in all areas of business. On this basis, business and academic writers and researchers agree that companies should embark on selective outsourcing to multiple vendors. The multiple vendor model could consist of one vendor acting as the prime contractor, or all vendors enjoying equal status. British Petroleum Exploration Operations Company (BPX), for example, pursued multiple and selective outsourcing contracts by outsourcing its IT requirements to three vendors, but appointed the strongest in the field of each of its three major regions as prime contractor. Other companies have adopted a similar approach. The Halliburton Co, a natural resources and energy company in Dallas, awarded ten-year outsourcing contracts, worth a total of \$500 million to Andersen Consulting for applications development, to I-Net for networking, and to Power Computing for mainframe operations. The Halliburton Co concluded that contracting with best-of-breed suppliers can not only promote higher quality service, but also reduce costs by as much as 10–15 per cent more than that provided by the one-stop-shop outsourcing giants. Benetton, the 'clothing service company' is widely quoted as having developed contract management capabilities as a core competence. Benetton now successfully manages more than 500 contractual relationships just in the Veneto region, north of Venice, where 80 per cent of its production takes place. The other 20 per cent of production is located outside Italy.

Other sourcing arrangements include joint ventures, cross equities and franchises. Virgin, whose interests encompass retailing, travel, soft drinks, music, amongst other business ventures, have entered into joint venture agreements, whereby they provide the brand name and marketing flair and the other parties, the production facilities and capital. In 1997 the Australian Commonwealth Bank (ACB) entered into a strategic partnership with Electronic Data Systems (EDS), a transaction reported to be worth A\$500 million a year for a period of ten years and involving ACB's purchase of 35 per cent equity stake in EDS, Australia. Yet certain joint ventures have not been so successful. For example, Delta's joint venture with TransQuest Information Solutions encountered a series of difficulties two years after it started and the partnership eventually dissolved.

An alternative form of outsourcing is spin-offs. Spin-offs are the result of exposing particular internal cost based activities to market forces; if successful, they are turned into separately managed profit centres. In effect, certain organisations develop world-class competences in supplementary or non-core activities that they, in turn, spin-off into separate organisations with the aim of making them a separate, profitable business.

A growing number of examples of firms are developing world class competences, particularly in IT, with the object of creating new IT products and services which are often unrelated to the parent's traditional line of business. An example is General Motors' spin-off of EDS, currently viewed as one of the most successful suppliers of IT services. Similarly, Mercedes-Daimler AG, now the DaimlerChrysler Group, in addition to its expertise for car manufacturing, developed world class competences in supporting activities such as IT, finance and telecommunications. As the IT function, in particular, was considered to be world class, Mercedes-Daimler AG decided to create a new service company, DaimlerChrysler Services (Debis) in order to turn its IT expertise into a profitable revenue stream. Thus, Debis Systemhaus GmbH, or Debis IT services, was established in 1990, as the computer-outsourcing subsidiary that undertook to source the IT needs of the parent company and also compete in the market place. Later on, two more market facing divisions were created, Debis Financial Services and Debis Telecom Services. Since its formation, Debis has grown to become Germany's leading independent provider of IT services, with an international presence in 32 countries and a portfolio that ranges from consulting services and software solutions to desktop services and the management of applications, data centres and communications.

Certain companies have formed spin-off, market facing units in cooperation with other commercial entities. For example, in 1995 Liberty National Bank and Trust (USA) created a subsidiary, Liberty Payment Services, to provide an overnight cheque clearing service for banks. Liberty's cheque processing capability, combined with the logistics capability of UPS Worldwide Logistics, achieved lower costs and speedier processing than that offered by the Federal Reserve System. Similarly, Holiday Inn structured its hotel reservations business as a separate entity based on its relationship with IBM's ISSC to serve the entire hotel and hospitality market. The Bank of Scotland has formed a joint venture spin-off, First Banking System (FIS), with the FI Group.* The 320 bank services staff and 120 staff from the FI Group make up the FIS organisation with a charter to provide commercial software development, IT systems planning and architecture to the bank, to a value of £150 million over five years.

Another, looser, form of sourcing arrangement is provisioned by alliances, consortia and shared service agreements. Strategic alliances, in particular, have been described as an 'in vogue' form of arrangement, often because they are seen as the most appropriate mechanism to bring together partners who entertain various, sometimes asymmetric and possibly conflicting objectives. Yet, irrespective of the reasons for the

---

*The FI Group is now known as Xansa.

formation of a strategic alliance, transparency between the partners is considered as the key to success. Policies that enhance information sharing, or the deployment of shielding mechanisms in order to protect key competences, aid the successful management of strategic alliances. Kodak, for example, pioneered outsourcing through strategic alliances by awarding five- and ten-year contracts in 1989 to IBM and Digital Equipment, now operating as Entex Information Services, with an estimated value of US$1.5 billion. The outsourcing agreements were structured both to allow the suppliers to achieve profit and also to encourage them to continuously improve the assets under their remit. Contracts contained neither formal incentives nor penalty clauses, but an understanding that if the suppliers performed well, Kodak would make greater use of their sourcing capabilities.

Organisations are also turning to consortia based sourcing, otherwise known as sourced service consortia, for the purposes of achieving greater economies of scale through outsourcing. For example, Gothaer Corporation, one of Germany's biggest insurance groups, first formed a joint venture with IBM Germany to handle all Gothaer's data processing, internal and external networks and the development of their applications software. Then, together with two other German insurance companies, Gothaer set up a joint venture company, or sourced service consortia arrangement, called Allegemeine Versicherungssoftware GmbH (General Insurance Software). The new company's mission is to create and market applications software based on standard architecture, such as IBM's Insurance Application Architecture, to other insurance companies. This venture combines insurance business process know-how with IBM's technical expertise. Similarly NV Philips, the Dutch electronic giant, first set up a joint venture, BSO-Origin, with 15 per cent equity share and two seats on the management board, with BSO Beheer, the Dutch software enterprise, to outsource its applications development function. Subsequently, Philips C&PS and BSO-Origin cooperated to deliver service jointly to external customers and later secured the cooperation of a few more software services providers. Ultimately, this venture extended its original commercial identity and became a sourced service consortia enterprise.

The Kakabadse survey

Ours predominantly is a straightforward relationship between the purchaser and us as the provider...Our problem with a joint venture...is the danger of pollution to the core competence and service

Box   *Continued*

product we as an organisation are achieving vs. the other parties' capabilities. So, for instance, whilst we would claim to be a market leader in the provision of nurses, doctors and other outcare employeees..., if someone said to us why don't you run the hospital porters and hospital security, we would say no...because we might well pollute our capability of running our services – Justin Jewitt, CEO, Nestor Healthcare Group Plc

The contractual and structural relationships that support outsourcing emerge from the survey as contrasting with the trends emerging from other studies (Figure 2.9). For service purchasers, and echoing the sentiments expressed by Justin Jewitt, the two most preferred sourcing arrangements are single contracts, in particular with trusted suppliers with whom there is already a relationship. The 'less traditional' contractual relationships, such as strategic alliances, contracts with multiple suppliers who are required to offer an integrated high quality service, flexible pricing contracts and various forms of partnerships, fall a long way behind the preferred supplier/single contract mode of operating. Shared sourcing

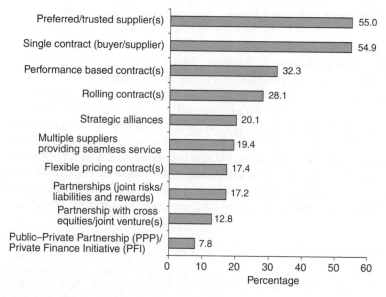

Figure 2.9   Sourcing arrangements.
Note: Respondents selected multiple options.

consortia type arrangements attracted such a low percentage of responses that they have been omitted from the presentation of results.

International comparison emphasises a similar trend, namely that of greater reliance on trusted suppliers and/or single contract relationships with service providers (Figure 2.10). European companies express a greater preference for single contract relationships with preferred and trusted suppliers. Although lower on the list of priorities, the more 'up beat' type contracts given so much attention in the literature are more favoured by European companies than by US firms. European companies prefer performance based, rolling and flexible pricing contracts and partnerships which share risks and involvement with multiple suppliers who display a capability for being sufficiently integrated to provide a seamless service.

Although low on the list of priorities, US companies indicate greater use of strategic alliances and partnerships based on cross equity participation than do European or UK companies. Although marginally more favoured by US companies, the shared sourcing consortium concept nevertheless is identified as one of the least preferred sourcing arrangements and is therefore omitted from the presentation of results.

Sourcing with whom?

Emerging trends

In the literature and in the popular press, certain service providers such as EDS, Andersen Consulting, IBM, Geddes, Science Application International Corporation (SAIC), KPNQuest, are identified as the preferred suppliers of outsourcing services.

Yet, as discussed earlier in this chapter (see Sourcing What), a relatively new type of outsourcing market entrant has emerged, namely organisations that offer IT hosting. The reason for the growing popularity for IT hosting enterprises is that many businesses are using the internet to eliminate the burden of buying and running expensive, complex information systems. Microsoft, for example, uses Exodus Communications for a wide range of services, particularly for playing host to corporate accounting, personnel and payroll programmes. Such a relationship also allows Microsoft immediate access to the world of e-commerce. As a result, and in addition to ASPs, a whole new class of service companies has begun to emerge, namely business service providers (BSPs) and computer service providers (CSPs). Application service providers such as Corio specialise in licensing, maintaining and the renting of software

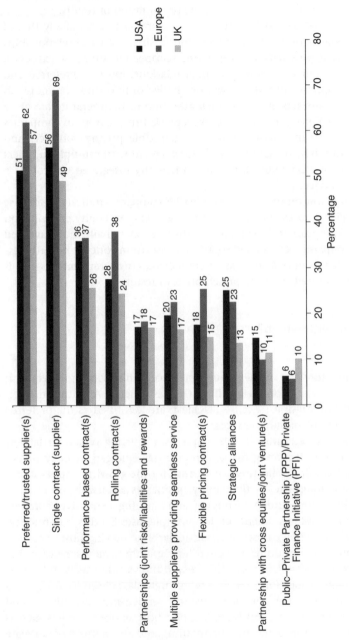

Figure 2.10 Nature of sourcing relationship: international comparison.
Note: Respondents selected multiple options.

systems, often accounting and human resources applications, written by third parties, for a broad range of business clients. Tibersoft, a BSP enterprise, has drafted software for the food-distribution industry, a software that connects vendors and restaurants. In effect, software has been tailored to meet the needs of one industry. Exodus Communications, a typical CSP, acts as a 'server farm' that houses equipment for ASPs, BSPs and e-commerce transactions, allowing customers to 'plug in' to their software. Other companies exploit market niches, for example EDS and Qwest, who have turned themselves into a combination of ASPs and CSPs in order to offer services to SAP, a German enterprise software vendor.

Others like Syntacom offer outsourcing services in such areas as work-flow management, data warehousing, data archiving, IT networking, web hosting and internet services. Together with their subsidiary Planet, Syntacom assists clients to generate strategies for developing and implementing appropriate IT infrastructures. For example, one of Planet Online's clients has been the Rover Group, the UK car manufacturer. Through Rover, Planet run one of the largest web data centres outside the United States of America. Besides having a core competence in web applications, Planet Online possesses the advantage of economies of scale, which the Rover Group cannot reproduce. Further studies support the view that enterprises are choosing from niche and speciality shops such as ASPs, web hosting and e-commerce providers, as well as network-integration experts. The options range from a complete handing over of IT operations by the host organisation to pay-as-you-go for a single application outsourcing.

The Kakabadse survey

> ...a lot more companies will sign up as sole suppliers...and the decision to appoint should probably be the biggest decision you've made. You should be very critical and very precise about the process you go through to appoint – Jim Leng, CEO, Laporte Plc

Again, the Kakabadse survey results portray a different picture from the one emerging from the business and academic literature. More in keeping with the views of Jim Leng, Figure 2.11 shows that most organisations strongly prefer suppliers with a proven track record and with particular industry sector experience. Niche providers and contracting with a relevant mix of providers form the third and fourth most preferred options. The more established service providers, such as EDS, Debis, the

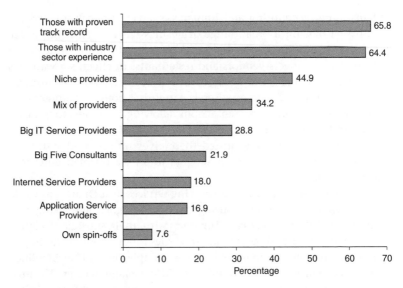

Figure 2.11   Preferred service providers.
Note: Respondents selected multiple options.

big five consultants (Andersens, KPMG, PWC, etc.), ISPs and ASPs, form the 'tail-end' of preferred suppliers.

International comparison of types of preferred suppliers emphasises a similar trend (Figure 2.12). European companies report a greater preference for utilising suppliers with relevant industry sector experience than US and UK companies. Further, US and European companies virtually equally prefer suppliers who have a proven track record. The remaining types of service providers are considerably less utilised than suppliers who can exhibit relevant industry sector experience and have a proven track record in particular specialisms. The UK companies indicate greater liking for arrangements with a mix of providers. Further, US companies display a greater propensity for using the larger IT service providers, the big five consultancies and ASPs, but such preferences are lower on their list of priorities. Spin-offs emerge as particularly low on the list of preferred service providers in contrast to the attention they have been given in the literature.

Employee arrangements

Emerging trends

The electronic revolution and the ever growing requirement by companies to differentiate themselves from competitors through strategies which

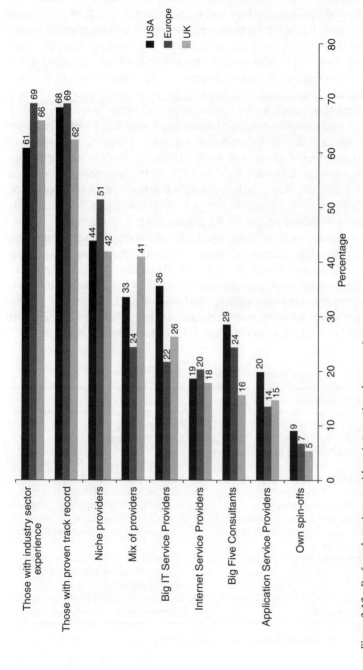

Figure 2.12 Preferred service providers: international comparison.
Note: Respondents selected multiple options.

provide a variety of cost and service quality advantages, have dramatically affected the shape of jobs and triggered a redesign in the way work is structured. Job based flexibility has become an imperative for organisations that are pursuing a combination of contrasting strategies, such as those intending to achieve economies of scale whilst improving standards of service delivery. Large enterprises in the United States of America, Canada, northern Europe and Australia are increasingly adopting limited term contracts, associate like relationships and home based teleworking, as a standard form of contractual relationship with employees. The prime reason for such developments is cost reduction. However, the individual is also considered to benefit from the more flexible arrangements, allowing greater disposable time. In 1998, in the European Union, there were 1.1 million people, approximately 0.8 per cent of the workforce, employed on such a basis. In the year 2000 this figure is estimated to stand at 4.4 million people, or 3.1 per cent of the workforce.

Organisations are increasingly 'externalising' the employment relationship through part-time, temporary, casual and fixed-term contractual arrangements, as a means of securing both cost advantage and labour flexibility. Such externalised work arrangements reflect a change of understanding in the relationship between employee and employer. The traditional psychological contract whereby employees acquire job security in exchange for 'loyalty' is changing to one of performance for reward (Table 2.2).

Table 2.2   Changing nature of the social contract

Old social contract	New social contract
• Employment	• Employability
• Job security	• Career resilience
• Corporation drives career structure	• Career portfolio. Self responsibility for designing career
• Corporate reliant employees	• Self-reliant employees
• Trust in corporation	• Trust in self and network
• Loyalty to corporation	• Loyalty to self, profession and network
• Commitment to corporation	• Personal flexibility and performance
• Limited availability of information to employees	• Disclosure of information to employees
• Corporation assesses training needs	• Corporation provides tools, and opportunities for assessing and developing skills
• Corporation provides training and development	• Individuals expand their skills to stay competitive

Source: Compiled from Kakabadse and Kakabadse (2000b).

The psychological contract that determines people's motivation to work and patterns of employment is changing. The traditional emphasis on employment is being replaced by considerations of employability. Loyalty and a career path in one organisation is giving way to job specialisation, supplemented by the skills to find work whenever needed. The employer's responsibility has switched from providing security and direction to offering individuals the opportunity to enhance their employment prospects. The pay-for-performance and career-resilience perspectives characterise a change of responsibility from reliance on the employer to provide developmental opportunities for the individual to employee based responsibility to look after one's own training and career progress. A number of writers argue that as a result employees no longer acknowledge the existence of a supportive social contract between themselves and their employer. Some take an extreme view, maintaining that employee commitment is 'all but gone' and can only be resuscitated when companies create a mutually beneficial working environment.

The Kakabadse survey

> ... in any successful organisation, covering for your people is a primary requirement. ... When it comes to outsourcing decisions, one of the issues will always be, what is the impact on the people who were previously handling the service – Graham Brown, Chief Operating Officer, National Power

The most favoured arrangement for employees affected by outsourcing is to transfer staff from the host organisation to the supplier (Figure 2.13). The second most preferred approach is to adopt a mixture of HR strategies to suit the particular circumstances of the outsourcing programme. A number of companies also report that outsourcing has no impact on the way people are managed or on the terms of contract employees have with their employer. Equally, outsourcing emerges as only marginally affecting the security of employment of staff, in that they are redeployed either within the host organisation or with suppliers. Many companies report the conditions of employment for staff and managers as not having been fundamentally changed. In contrast, a minority of companies do highlight more basic changes to employment conditions as over 25 per cent of the respondents report redundancies. The least common arrangement for employees is redeployment with new terms of conditions of employment. The trend is towards keeping people

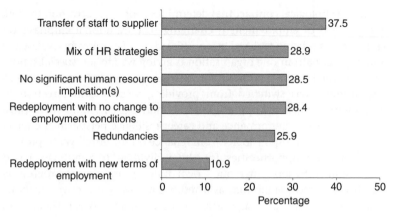

Figure 2.13   Outsourcing impact on employee arrangements.
Note: Respondents selected multiple options.

or redeploying them, but with little or no change to their contracts. Graham Brown's advice to 'care for your people' seems to be heeded by many senior managers.

International comparison of the arrangements that are made for employees affected by outsourcing supports a trend comparable to that reported in Figure 2.13. In US, UK and European companies the most preferred HR strategy arising from outsourcing initiatives is the transfer of staff to suppliers (Figure 2.14). Many UK companies also report that outsourcing has no significant impact on current employee contractual arrangements. In contrast, European companies highlight that outsourcing has a significant impact on human resource management and employee contractual arrangements. European companies report a higher level of redundancy arising from outsourcing initiatives than in US and UK companies. As well as redundancies, European companies favour the redeployment of staff from the host organisation to the service provider but with no change to their conditions of employment. Alternatively, US and UK companies prefer to adopt a mix of HR strategies that suit the particular requirements of the firm. Although the Kakabadse survey results confirm that oursourcing leads to changes for employees, as less than 30 per cent of responses indicate that the current human resource policies and practices will be maintained, the overall trend emphasises change of employer, but not necessarily change of contract. Other than redundancies, contractual obligations are maintained but with a new host organisation.

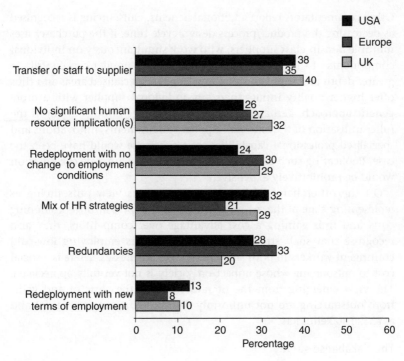

Figure 2.14 Outsourcing impact on employee arrangements: international comparison.
Note: Respondents selected multiple options.

Sourcing outcomes

Emerging trends

As already identified, the Kakabadse survey shows that outsourcing offers several advantages to the host organisation. The key benefits are:

- enabling the senior management of the enterprise to focus on core activities;
- providing the means for achieving the key strategic objectives of the organisation;
- promoting cost advantage whilst simultaneously introducing a cost discipline mentality into the organisation;
- providing a means for improving quality of service;
- having senior management consider the advantages of increasing their investment in technology.

Other commentators report additional benefits. Outsourcing is recognised as decreasing the product/process design cycle time, if the purchaser uses multiple best-in-class suppliers, who work simultaneously on individual components of the system. On this basis, each supplier can contribute greater depth and sophisticated knowledge in specialised areas and thus offer higher quality inputs than any individual supplier with a more generic approach. Perhaps the greatest advantage of outsourcing is the fuller utilisation of the external suppliers' investments, innovations and specialised professional capabilities than otherwise would have been the case. Replicating such an array of competences in any one organisation would be prohibitively expensive.

On the other hand, although certain writers view outsourcing as representing state-of-the art management in the pursuit of repositioning costs and thus gaining a cost advantage over competitors, they also recognise that such strategies can create sectors employing low-paid contingent workers in both small and larger businesses. There is a social cost to outsourcing whose impact on society is not yet fully appreciated. The view emerging from the literature is that the costs of and gains from outsourcing are not uniformly distributed amongst internal and external stakeholders.

The Kakabadse survey

The survey lists the outsourcing outcomes which service purchasers and service providers consider as critical. These outcomes range from the enhancing of cost advantage to the realisation of opportunity gains (Figure 2.15). The results emphasise that well-managed programmes of outsourcing increase operational effectiveness in the organisation, allow for better utilisation of in-house staff and help senior management to more concentrate on the core competences of the organisation in order to realise competitive advantage. The commonly quoted criticism of outsourcing, that it lowers staff morale, is supported. The survey results indicate that outsourcing leads to a marginal reduction in staff, accompanied by a pronounced decrease in staff motivation. The 'new psychological contract' is not held in high esteem by most of the respondents involved in outsourcing initiatives, despite the fact that the results presented in Figures 2.13 and 2.14 show far more redeployment of staff than redundancies. The anxieties concerned with change seem to induce substantial demotivation.

A similar pattern of results emerges when comparing US, UK and European companies (Figure 2.16). European companies report positive experiences concerning the impact of cost reduction exercises. They

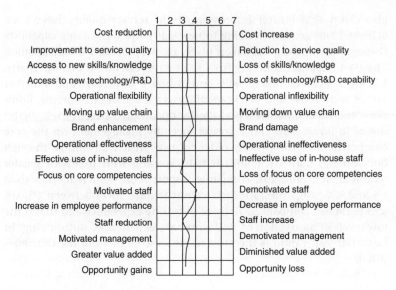

Figure 2.15 Outsourcing outcomes.

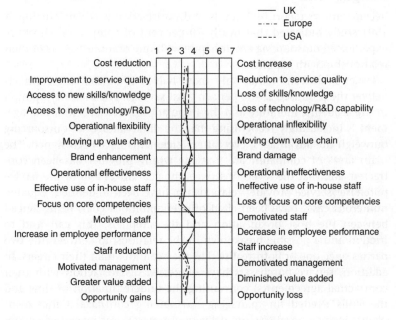

Figure 2.16 Outsourcing outcomes: international comparison.

also claim that greater improvements in service quality have been achieved and greater accessing to new skills and technology capability through outsourcing has taken place, than by US and UK companies. The US companies, differing from their European and UK counterparts, highlight a greater loss of skills and in-house knowledge and a further loss of technology and R&D capability as a result of outsourcing. European and US companies report greater operational effectiveness, better use of in-house staff and a greater focus by management on the core competences of the firm in order to gain greater advantage through outsourcing, than UK companies. In keeping with trends of greater redundancies, European companies report more staff reduction than US and UK companies. Irrespective of the differences between US, UK and European companies, all three share one experience and that is the low levels of motivation of staff who have experienced outsourcing. In fact, staff motivation is the most negative score of all of the outcomes listed.

Sourcing satisfaction

Emerging trends

Recent surveys report high levels of dissatisfaction with outsourcing. A 1991 study indicated that nearly 70 per cent of companies who have experienced outsourcing are unhappy with one or more aspects of their relationship with suppliers.

Other studies show that only about half of IT outsourcing contracts deliver the promised 20–30 per cent cost savings. The majority opinion in the academic literature and the popular press is that senior management is increasingly recognising that the disadvantages of outsourcing outweigh the advantages, even after agreements have been signed. The main areas of complaint are that the wrong provider has been contracted, and that the levels of service, the guarantees and/or the service purchaser/service provider relationship, have been ill-defined. Equally, numerous cases have been cited of over-ambitious goals being agreed between the host organisation and the suppliers; this can lead to friction and a possible breakdown in the relationship between the two parties once one or both realise that they cannot attain their targets. In addition, service purchasers have expressed dissatisfaction with their contractual agreement(s) concerning the underestimation of time and the skills needed for managing outsourcing contracts. Other complaints include unsatisfactory delivery of services, uncooperative vendor

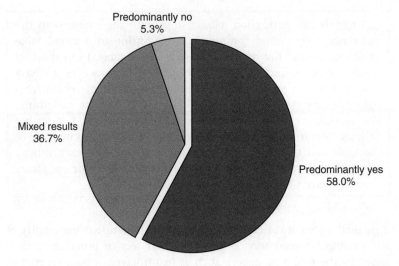

Figure 2.17 Sourcing satisfaction.

behaviour, the cost of the service being too high, and/or the competitive advantage of outsourcing no longer exists. Although there is evidence that some vendors do perform poorly, equally there is evidence that poor outsourcing decisions are the direct result of an inadequate definition of customer requirements by the customers themselves. Thus, although many companies are attempting to conceal the failure of their outsourcing agreements by, for example, taking IT back in-house, or hiring back staff to provide an in-house service, such errors are increasingly being identified as costly and embarrassing.

The Kakabadse survey

In contrast to the more negative trends reported by other writers, the survey reports positive experiences of outsourcing (Figure 2.17). Despite accounts by other writers of higher levels of staff demotivation, 58 per cent of the respondents indicate that they are satisfied with their outsourcing arrangements. Over 36 per cent of respondents indicate mixed feelings as to what they have gained from outsourcing and less than 6 per cent report dissatisfaction with their experience of outsourcing. Virtually identical results emerge from an international comparison (Figure 2.18). Senior managers from European companies report greater satisfaction with outsourcing, whilst senior managers of UK companies emphasise more negative experiences.

> Right from the start, good relationships with the client, with the purchaser – very good communications! Sitting in a round table environment and not on opposite sides of the table. I can think of the very first contract we ever did in one specific aspect of the NHS (national health service) where we had an excellent relationship right from the start where we were both trying to create something. We worked very well, ... with weekly meetings and monthly reviews. Within three months we were all sitting on the same side of the table and had a level of trust and enjoyment of each other's achievements. It worked very well for us as a template for our future – Justin Jewitt, CEO, Nestor Healthcare Group Plc

A particular area of concern identified in the literature is the quality of relationship between service purchaser and service provider. Clearly stated by the senior managers, such as Justin Jewett, who took part in the Kakabadse survey, is that the relationships between service purchasers and service providers depends on the quality of the relationship management skills exhibited by the staff and management in both organisations. The attitudes displayed towards outsourcing, in general, and service providers, in particular, and the morale of staff and management involved in the contract also have an important bearing on the success of the sourcing relationship. It is the balance between the relationship requirements and the relationship management capabilities of both service purchasers and service providers that determines the level of integration between the parties involved. The Kakabadse survey

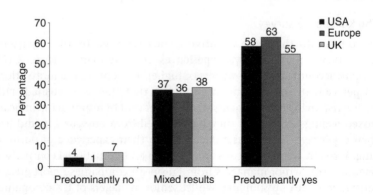

Figure 2.18   Sourcing satisfaction: international comparison.

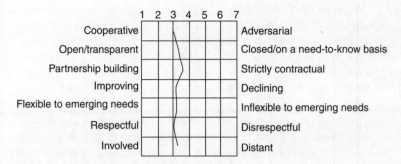

Figure 2.19 Quality of sourcing relationship(s).

indicates that positive relationships exist between service purchasers and service providers (Figure 2.19).

The survey trends characterise the relationships between the host organisation and supplier(s) as being cooperative and respectful.

The quality of sourcing relationships between the host organisation and service providers, as reported by US, UK and European companies supports the positive perspective identified in Figure 2.19. The US, UK and European companies indicate that a helpful and respectful relationship has been negotiated between service purchasers and service providers, sufficiently flexible to adapt to changes that arise with either partners and with their contractual obligations (Figure 2.20). European companies, in particular, display that they have established more cooperative, transparent, and better integrated relationships between service purchasers and service providers than US and UK companies.

These findings support the trends identified in Figures 2.9 and 2.10. Current practice is for service purchasers to form strong business ties

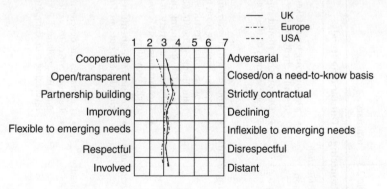

Figure 2.20 Quality of sourcing relationship(s): international comparison.

Table 2.3 Summary

Outsourcing	Outsourcing trends	The Kakabadse survey
Considerations Reason	• Outsourcing undertaken for reasons of cost discipline/reduction	• Mix of reasons for outsourcing
Purpose	• Outsourcing should support the core competences of the organisation	• Differences of trend by region. European companies more concerned with cost discipline/control concerns. The US firms more focused on achieving best practice and improving service quality.
Arrangements	• A mix of sourcing arrangements is becoming more popular, ranging from relationships with multiple vendors, joint ventures with cross equities, franchising, spin-offs, alliances, sourced service consortia, and hiring the services of internet and ASP's under a variety of contractual arrangements • Greatest emphasis is on IT service providers and niche providers	• Two predominant forms of sourcing arrangements emerge, those with preferred and trusted suppliers and single contracts with suppliers • Greatest preference is for those service providers with a proven track record and those with relevant industry sector experience • European companies prefer relationships with favoured niche suppliers and on a single contract basis
Sourcing area	• Considerable attention has been given to the growth of IT outsourcing	• Basic services, HR and IT are identified as the three key areas of outsourcing • UK companies more than US and European companies identify basic services as a key area for outsourcing
Criticality	• Central to the development of the enterprise • Level of criticality varies according to sourcing purposes, polarised as cost reduction or leveraging core competences	• Central to the development of the enterprise • Different reasons are identified for undertaking outsourcing which range from reduction of costs for the purposes of gaining a cost advantage,

	• The capability to manage outsourcing contracts is equally considered as critical to the success of outsourcing programmes	• to improving service quality and striving to achieve best practice • Any programme of outsourcing may be undertaken for different objectives which are pursued simultaneously • The capability to integrate numerous outsourcing strategies which are running concurrently and which may not have a good 'fit' between them is considered crucial to the success of the programme • The processes, activities, and functions outsourced are perceived as more critical to the future development of UK companies • US companies consider those areas outsourced as having more of a commodity status
Satisfaction	• Higher levels of dissatisfaction than satisfaction are reported with outsourcing • Service purchasers report greater dissatisfaction with outsourcing • Outsourcing generates low wage contingent workers • Outsourcing leads to staff reductions • The longer term social impact of outsourcing is not yet appreciated	• Satisfaction with the value gained from outsourcing is reported • European companies report higher levels of satisfaction from outsourcing than do UK and US companies • Outsourcing leads to staff reduction • Outsourcing leads to greater staff demotivation
Decision to outsource	• An increasing number of outsourcing decisions are taken at board/senior manager level	• Most decisions are taken at board and executive committee levels • In European companies, most outsourcing decisions are taken at board level • In US companies, the greater number of outsourcing decisions are taken at senior manager level

with service providers who have relevant industry sector experience and/or those with a proven track record in particular niche areas. The more successful the relationship, the more likely positive interdependencies will be forged between service purchaser and service provider. Working on making the service purchaser/provider relationship more collaborative and more effective avoids the need to switch suppliers. European companies seem to be more successful in forming robust relationships with their suppliers than US and UK companies.

Summary

The material in this chapter is summarised in Table 2.3

References and further reading

This chapter has compared the trends in outsourcing practice identified by business and academic writers with the results of the Kakabadse survey. Seven key areas were examined, namely, the reasons for outsourcing, what is being outsourced, how sourcing relationships are being managed, the service providers that are most and least preferred service purchasers, the arrangements made for employees affected by outsourcing, the impact of, and satisfaction with, outsourcing. Further reading in these areas, particularly for providing reference and further information on the case examples mentioned in the chapter, is given in the following section.

Sourcing reasons

For further information on:

- The concept of competences or the core competencies of an organisation, read Prahalad and Hamel (1990), Peisch (1995) and Mullin (1996).
- Being sensitive and responsive to market demands, read Willcocks and Fitzgerald (1993; 1994).
- Core and peripheral activities, read Quinn and Hilmer (1994) and Alexander and Young (1996).
- Competitive advantage, read Porter (1985; 1990), Brueck (1995), Chalos and Sung (1998) and Quinn (1999).
- Scale and cost advantage reasons for outsourcing, read Finlay and King (1999), Currie and Willcocks (1997) and the National Computing Centre reports (1999a; 1999b).
- The impact of global competitive pressures, read Grant (1995), Domberger (1998), DiRomualdo and Gurbaxani (1998).

- Managerial incentives, read Willamson (1988; 1996) and Chalos and Sung (1998).

For further information on:

- Argyle Diamonds and Apple Computers, see Quinn and Hilmer (1994).
- Unilever's slimline portfolio strategy, see Willman (1999).
- Chrysler's 'SCORE' strategy, see Christian (1997) and Chalos and Sung (1998).
- General Motors suppliers' warranty costs initiative, see Blumenstein (1997); for an overview of outsourcing in the auto industry, read Cusumano and Takeishi (1991).
- DaimlerChrysler and Andersen's relationship, see Van Laarhoven et al. (1999).

Sourcing what

For further information on:

- Information technology outsourcing, read Narin (1999), Dyer and Ouchi (1993) and Murray and Kotabe (1999).
- 'best in breed' IT outsourcing, read the Gartner Group (1999) and IDC (1999).
- Business process management (BPM), read Jones (1994) and Foremski (1999).
- The Hewlett-Packard case study, see Forester Research Inc. (1999).
- Internet Service Providers (ISPs), see Forester Research Inc. (1999).

Sourcing how

For further information on:

- Service purchaser/service provider relationships, read Bensaou (1999) and Cross (1995); for the development of such relationships in the field of operations research, Murray and Kotabe (1999).
- Multiple vendor and network contract based relationships, read Currie and Willcocks (1997), Miles and Snow (1994; 1997) and Venkatraman and Loh (1994).
- Joint ventures, cross equities and franchises, read Domberger (1998) and Narin (1999).
- Spin-offs, read Chalos and Sung (1998).

- Alliances, consortia and the concept of shared services, read Lei and Slocum (1992) and Inkpen and Beamish (1997).

Sourcing with whom

For further information on developments with EDS, Andersen Consulting, IBM, Geddes, SAIC, KPNQuest, ASPs, BSPs and CSP's, read Nee (1999), Klein (1999) and Teresko (1999).

Employee arrangements

For further information on:

- Current and future developments in human resource management, read Tyson and York (2000); Torrington and Hall (1998), Mishra and Mishra (1994) and Mishra, Spreitzer and Mishra (1998).
- Teleworking, read Standen et al. (1999).
- New ways of working in the European Union, read Tregaskis (1999) and Sparrow (2000).
- How to increase labour flexibility, read Korac-Kakabadse et al. (1999) and Purcell (1996).
- Arguments in favour of and against the old and new psychological and social contract, read Moskal (1993), Morrison (1994), Rousseau (1989), Greller (1994), Kakabadse and Kakabadse (2000b), Mills (1996) and Mone (1994).

Sourcing outcomes

For further information on:

- The impact and value of outsourcing, read Quinn (1999), Harrison (1994) and Hall and Domberger (1995).
- The levels of satisfaction with outsourcing, particularly in relation to the 70 per cent dissatisfaction, read Lacity et al. (1995). Also see Currie and Willcocks (1999), Moran (1999), Forst (1999) and Kessler et al. (1999).

3
Best Practice

Case study: best practice considerations

Interview with David Scotland, Chief Executive Officer (CEO) Allied Domecq

Interviewer:	What are the primary motives for outsourcing?
Scotland:	...the first critical review has to be strategic, what business are we in? Which things do we need to do ourselves so that we can, hopefully, create a difference, but also be excellent on those specifics which we know are the ones that cause us to succeed?
Interviewer:	This leads to the development of core competences in the organisation?
Scotland:	Yes, definitely. The strategic intention should inform your view of the core competences and I would take a view that you should almost start from the, 'why do we need it?' – rather than the 'why do we not need it?' – so savings should not be the imperative that informs you most of all but rather a clear strategy for sustainable growth.
Interviewer:	How much value added has been gained from out-sourcing arrangements?
Scotland:	I definitely come back to strategy again. I think if a company has decided that the business they are really in is the operations core competences, then you can add

Box   *Continued*

value by outsourcing things that are not essential to that core competence. I think if it's done right a lot of value is added and is sustainable because the experts in those fields will have to keep constantly renewing their skills, their systems, their management...We can expect from them a constant updating of their approach...but its not something we would take in-house. That kind of thing adds value...you can only decide what is muscle and what is fat if you know what type of body you want to be. Strategy is my answer to your question!

Interviewer: Yesterday, a top director told me that he would out-source everything except leadership; what do you think?

Scotland: I think fundamentally the same. Leadership and making strategy real, exciting and engaging to people...If a leader is leading without a sense of where something is going it's not sustainable...It's terribly important that the organisation retains control of the culture they want and clearly indicates where the organisation is...and where it wants to be. I also believe, however, that you need a real team around the core competence of the organisation.

Interviewer: You mean that control of any outsourced activity should be kept in-house?

Scotland: Absolutely and it's the same with the things that we all outsource, which is advertising agencies. You can get to a situation with an advertising agency that they would like to do your marketing. Thus, for an organisation like ours which realises its real value from marketing, it would be a disaster. If you give an advertising agency... an international review of your brands, the next step almost inevitably, if you permit it, is that they will manage the brand. That's not right.

Interviewer: Are we seeing a wave of consciousness from consumers?

Scotland: Absolutely, I'm saying this from my experience...and I'm talking about...standard Scottish whisky, this must conform to the law...so it must come from Scotland. Who bottles it is often not really important...But you must find the truth of what consumers outwardly feel and believe... Now if we go to a brand like Laphroaig which comes from a small Scottish island, and is very special and exotic, like a Leica camera or a Bugatti car which is hand made and crafted, the consumer's extremely interested in where it comes from, who made it and the fact that the Prince of Wales is very happy because we've cleaned rivers and salmon swim in them – this is absolutely part of that brand...

Interviewer: One can see the downside of outsourcing, such as the use of child labour, loss of control and/or loss of quality.

Scotland: Now we are moving into sustainability, I think this is really interesting. I think people need to think longer term on this because if we are going to put our computer centre in Bombay because labour is very cheap... how long will those rates be the same? And what do you then do, suddenly move everything to Central Africa because it's cheaper? I have a problem with that. I don't think it's sustainable. I also happen, personally, to think it is not moral... I think you could end up missing your main strategic point if you are constantly making cynical and short-term profit gains by, basically, abusing poverty. There's another perspective that says if we take a long term investment view of this country, we believe this country is going to be part of the modern world... from a social point of view which means we will help to invest in schools... but if you are constantly looking, where can we get this labour cheapest, then you're going to run out of places.

Interviewer: What skills/competences does one need to successfully manage an outsourcing supplier?

Scotland: You need to be very clear about what you are outsourcing. You also need to be quite open about what may happen on projects... in all the mistakes we ever made, there were many on communication. If we had used consultants in the sourcing of IT, we would have had results faster. I am now convinced that it should be out sourced to specialists because of their flexibility and design capability. In-house, they are hierarchical... they

Box   *Continued*

> do not challenge so much, they are frightened of their
> bosses ... If we had gone to real experts in IT, we would
> have got the answers quicker. Therefore leadership
> is terribly important ... communication is absolutely
> essential. I think involvement is terribly important. ...
> There needs to be intense honesty. There has to be a
> leader who says it's safe to admit you are not perfect.

David Scotland's interview covers a variety of topics, including the reasons for outsourcing, determining outsourcing priorities, strategic sustainability, who controls branding and the morality of corporate behaviour. One theme permeates the discussion, namely, the leadership necessary to define the purpose of the company, to define what is added value and thereby differentiate the enterprise from its competitors, to define the strategies the company should pursue and hence the purpose and contribution of outsourcing. David Scotland insists that leaders need to be powerful communicators. They need to be honest and respected. Leaders who display such qualities create the platform for a well integrated, high-performing organisation. Clearly David Scotland regards strong leadership as a prerequisite to successful outsourcing.

In this chapter we examine how high-performance leadership affects best practice outsourcing. We pay attention to team-based leadership. As only a minority of companies emerge from the survey as exhibiting best practice, we compare high- and average-performing companies on different aspects of outsourcing. We identify the key areas for outsourcing best practice and look at the differences between high- and average-performing companies in terms of outcomes and value gained from outsourcing.

The 69 club

The Kakabadse survey identifies 69 companies out of the sample of 747 organisations as exhibiting best practice outsourcing as a result of one distinguishing feature, top class leadership. The most important aspect of leadership is the degree to which there exists a shared understanding and commitment at top management levels to the strategic direction being pursued by the organisation and to the value being gained from outsourcing (Figure 3.1).

Hence, what distinguishes high-performing from average-performing companies is the degree of cohesion at senior management levels

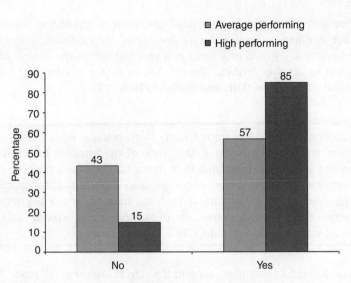

Figure 3.1 Shared view at the top: value from outsourcing.

concerning the identity with and commitment to pursue the vision and agreed strategies of the enterprise. The survey results show that team-based leadership is a key consideration in implementing sourcing strategies, whether they involve outsourcing or insourcing.

Top teams

Team-based leadership is a relatively recent concept. The more traditional approaches to understanding leadership have involved,

- analysing the characteristics of great leaders;
- distinguishing leadership tasks from other tasks and activities.

The enquiry into the nature, orientation and behaviours of great leaders has been going on for, virtually, as long as humankind has been in existence. Some writers consider that there are leadership attributes deeply ingrained in the person. The presumption is that such people are gifted, in that their 'born with' qualities set them apart. Others present a contrasting picture of leaders, namely as people who early in their life did not display any particular strengths. Their progress to greatness resulted from continuously wanting to learn. Some would consider the flair for vision and the passion for communication as elements of personality that cannot be trained for, even in childhood. However, other attributes – such as being disciplined, dependable, trustworthy and practical – would be viewed as learnt and within the control of the person to develop further. The conclusion is that outstanding leaders exhibit a mixture of skills and qualities (Table 3.1).

> ...because my career started really from being a soldier and from years and years of being at the front of the business in terms of service and marketing, and from being at the real interface with suppliers and customers, only coming into senior management quite late, and without any formal business training at the beginning, certain things have become clear to me concerning what it takes to be a leader – David Scotland, CEO, Allied Domecq

David Scotland's comments support the view of leaders as self made. Scotland emphasises the powerful experience of learning leadership through interacting with different stakeholder groups. Others highlight learning from mistakes or developing a discipline that spawns a clear mindedness coupled with a passion that inspires others to pursue key goals.

The alternative approach to analysing the characteristics of great leaders has been to examine the core tasks of leadership, so that those in command can decide what is required of them in order to perform effectively. A similar mix of skills, attributes, qualities and job-related requirements emerge when differentiating leadership tasks from man-

Table 3.1 Leadership skills and qualities

- Wisdom through experience
- Maturity through listening
- Behaving ethically through reflection
- Making judgements, not being judgmental
- Visioning through clarity of perspective
- Communicating through sensitivity to context
- Creative
- Trusting as a philosophy
- Sensitively discerning how and when to intervene
- Disciplined to be consistent and dependable
- Positive in outlook which promotes confidence in others
- Success oriented and energetic
- Enquiring through continuous learning
- Drive for follow through

Source: Compiled by authors.

Table 3.2 Leadership tasks

- Clarify vision
- Articulate/reflect values
- Motivate others
- Set clear goals
- Lead by example
- Create risk taking environment
- Nurture growth of intellectual capital
- Develop people/develop teams/invest in people
- Help others focus on task or goals
- Be sensitive to context
- Listen and attract feedback
- Exhibit passion for achievement
- Promote culture of responsibility and accountability

Source: Compiled by authors.

agerial or other types of tasks. Certain tasks, such as goal setting and motivating people to improve their performance, clearly stand apart as the activities required of a leader (Table 3.2). From there on, a mix of concepts emerges intermingling individual attributes with tasks to be done. The reason for such intertwining is that in order to undertake particular tasks, leaders need to display particular qualities so that others will trust them and follow them in the pursuit of certain goals. What leaders need to do, are required to do, what they chose to do, how they go about doing it and the qualities and attributes necessary for so doing, have become interlocked.

The main reason for the intertwining of individual leadership qualities and skills and leadership tasks is the influence of context. In different companies and in different circumstances, the attributes and qualities required of leaders, and the tasks they need to fulfil, will be different. In fact, in today's dynamic circumstances what is demanded of leaders even in different parts of the same organisation may vary substantially, generating internal tensions and frictions. Hence, understanding how to enhance leadership performance, a distinction needs to be made between the concept of leadership and the dynamics of context.

> ...my vision of what we could do was very clear...the concentration on quality indicators and focus. What McKinsey did was to guide us through the right questions and then answer those questions... this was always applied to the actual teams who do these things. At the beginning, we made a conscious decision with McKinsey to

Box   *Continued*

> choose the route of changing our people rather than hire and fire
> people. That was such a good decision because you then have learning
> groups. If we take a person from Spain onto the French project,
> somebody from Hungary onto the Dutch project, a vocabulary was
> formed, and, most importantly, a very open sense of progress – David
> Scotland, CEO, Allied Domecq

David Scotland is describing a context of learning, unique to the European operation of Allied Domecq. He also went on to describe the
application of learning in the workplace as, '. . . so much learning came
out of this learning'. In effect, creating a learning environment enabled
people to act on their own initiative. David Scotland also identifies that
learning takes place in teams. Taking people from different national
locations and bringing them together in a learning group in order to
appreciate how to enhance alignment in the organisation, links learning with leading the organisation through a philosophy of teamwork.
What Scotland is describing is the third and only recently explored
approach to understanding leadership, the concept of team-based or
discretionary leadership.

It was Professor Elliott Jaques's insightful contribution, in his analysis
of the Glacier Metal Company, that distinguished between managerial
roles that he described as prescriptive and those leadership roles he called
discretionary. Prescribed managerial roles are structured, with clear
boundaries, leaving the individual little room to exercise judgement.
More than half of such a role is predetermined (prescribed) in relation
to the tasks that need to be completed and how these tasks should be
performed. In contrast, a discretionary role is one where more than half
is shaped by its occupant. The individual's view of what needs to be
done and how it should be done determines the nature and structure of
that role. On this basis a prescribed role is more of a structured middle
management job, whereas a discretionary role is one that requires its
occupant to act as a leader and stamp his/her personality and philosophy
on that position (Figure 3.2).

Discretionary leaders need to determine the boundaries of their role
according to their vision for the organisation, function or activity for
which they are accountable. Such a challenge is virtually impossible to
meet unless the person has some sort of sense of what they are doing,
what will be their contribution and what value their function or activity
will add to the rest of the organisation. Take the information systems

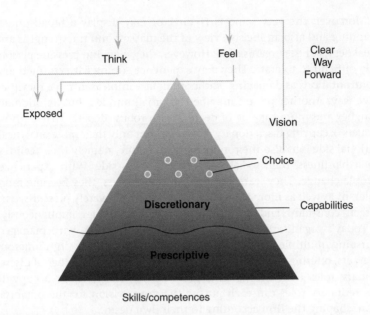

Figure 3.2 Discretionary leadership.
Source: Adapted from Kakabadse and Kakabadse 1999.

(IS/IT) function. One conclusion to have emerged from the extensive Cranfield studies on leadership and top teams is that high-performing organisations have an IS/IT function closely aligned with senior management and the board of directors. The reason? – so that change can be implemented across the organisation in a manner that is appropriate to the information needs of the different parts of the organisation. In such circumstances, the leadership ability of the IS/IT director is an important consideration. The IS/IT director, in deciding the nature and shape of his/her job and the configuration of the IS/IT function, would need to form a view of the various market and economic forces at play and from that perspective design an IS/IT department that will offer an added-value contribution to the rest of the organisation. The person would need to think seriously about what they are doing and why. A poor quality IS/IT director is evident, as his or her ability to discern between alternatives and identify a way forward is functionally oriented. They would instinctively want to adopt the latest technology on behalf of the organisation. This displays their orientation – they think as an IS/IT manager, but in a director's job. Hence, the manner in which someone discusses, analyses and projects their views reveals their leadership or management orientation.

Moreover, the very same IS/IT director may display a broad under-standing and also an incisive view of the markets and the strengths and weaknesses of the organisation. However, they may find pressure person-ally difficult to tolerate. They may experience coping with conflicts and confrontations as damaging. Rather than face unpleasantness, they may give way. Another person may be less broad minded, but emotionally tougher and more capable of dealing with robust debate. Hence, those leaders occupying discretionary roles show not only their more analytical, rational side, but also their more emotive nature, namely their feelings, their hardiness, their sociability, or their softer side. With experience, people change. They learn to progress, they regress, they become more tolerant as well as more intolerant, particularly if severely pressurised by targets, constraints and having to work on many activities simultaneously.

Today's organisations consist of complex structures, with managers pursuing multiple agendas. Many companies operate in numerous markets, offering contrasting products and services. A number of discre-tionary roles exist in any enterprise. Theoretically, those occupying discretionary roles can each pursue their own vision for the organisa-tion, shaping the firm according to their own desire.

Such visions may be capable of being easily integrated or may sharply contrast one with the other. Equally, the discretionary leaders in the organisation may share one vision, but their relationships may be strained, thus projecting strife and a lack of trust and exhibiting dysfunctional behaviour. The spread of discretionary roles may not be concentrated at the top. Managers in top positions, namely chairmen, CEOs and the other directors, occupy discretionary leadership roles. However, an organisation geared to providing high levels of service may well have younger managers in important client account roles who also occupy discretionary positions. Although much more junior, these managers may well exercise a substantial influence on the company. If one or more key client accounts are disrupted, the loss in revenue and the damage to external credibility could injure the standing of the enterprise. Hence, discretionary leaders affect strategy, positively through pursuing their vision and negatively by their capacity to undermine and damage what exists.

Thus, discretionary leadership analysis highlights the dynamic nature of how people interact within teams, with others across the organisation and with key stakeholders outside their organisation. High-performing dis-cretionary leaders display their capabilities. In contrast, high-performing staff and managers in prescriptive roles exhibit their skills and compe-tences. The reason for such difference is that discretionary leaders need to address the question, 'how capable are you of applying your skills and competences in this place today? In the last job you were in you may have been great! In the next job you go to, you may be superb. But what can you do here, today?' The measure of performance for discretionary leaders is capability, emphasising the contextual nature of leadership in private and public service organisations.

Top class outsourcing

The results captured on Figure 3.1 show that best practice outsourcing stems from senior management sharing a cohesive view concerning the value to be gained from pursuing outsourcing initiatives. Leadership is the one factor that distinguishes those companies who are effective at managing outsourcing programmes from those that are average performers. No significant difference in outsourcing capability emerges as a result of size of organisation measured by the total number of employees in the firm (Figure 3.3), the level of seniority of managers (Figure 3.4) or the age of managers (Figure 3.5). International comparison between US, UK and European companies shows no significant differences in the clarity and cohesiveness of view at senior levels concerning the value to be

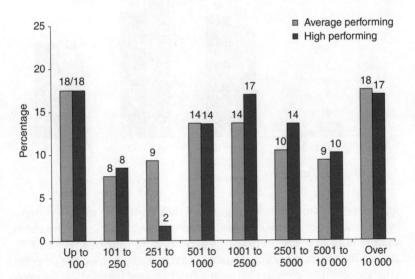

Figure 3.3 Total employees.

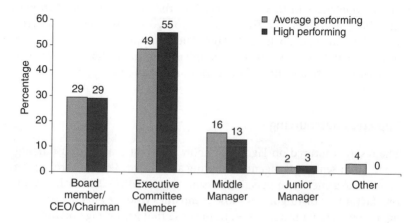

Figure 3.4   Level by organisation type.

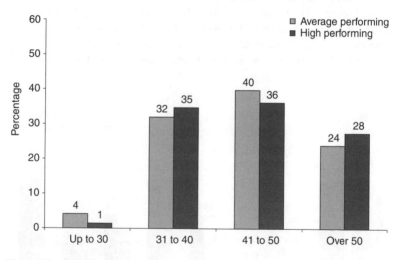

Figure 3.5   Age of managers.

gained, or not, from outsourcing (Figure 3.6). Further, managers in high- and average-performing companies report that they have comparable discretion to purchase outsourcing services from suppliers (Figure 3.7). In fact, managers enjoy considerable discretion to purchase the outsourcing services they consider necessary. International comparison between US, UK and European companies again emphasises the considerable

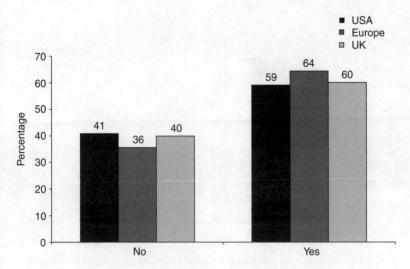

Figure 3.6   Shared view at the top: international comparison.

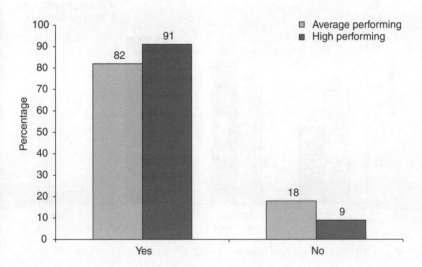

Figure 3.7   Discretion to purchase outsourcing services.

discretionary freedom available to management to purchase outsourcing services (Figure 3.8). In short, the results show a close similarity
between high- and average-performing companies, except for one factor,
the quality of top-team leadership.

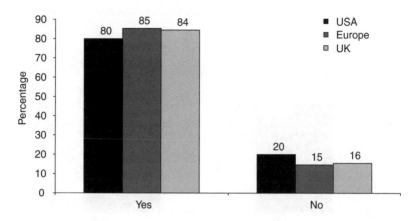

Figure 3.8   Discretion to purchase outsourcing services: international comparison.

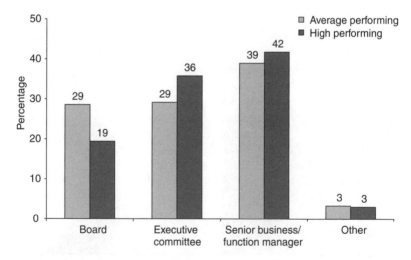

Figure 3.9   Initiation of decision to outsource.

The high-performing companies identified through the Kakabadse survey highlight five-core capabilities for conducting effective outsourcing, namely,

1   learning to trust your managers;
2   helping the organisation to become outsource ready;
3   developing the ability to pursue concurrent sourcing strategies;

4 developing the skills for managing details;
5 forming value adding relationships with different service providers.

Trusting your managers

> I think, in a way, it [outsourcing] has to be driven from the board down. If companies take strategy seriously – and most major companies that I'm involved with have a strategy meeting once a year where these kinds of things are discussed – outsourcing has to be a top down exercise rather than coming from below. It has to be driven by the CEO, by the top people – Sir Nigel Rudd, Chairman, Pilkingtons, plc; Chairman, Williams plc

Sir Nigel Rudd's view is that outsourcing is of such importance that it needs to be discussed at board level, and has to be driven by the CEO and the senior management of the enterprise. In effect, he suggests that outsourcing decisions are best made by the directors and senior general managers of the enterprise, so that outsourcing initiatives are implemented in a consistent and disciplined manner.

The Kakabadse survey supports Rudd's view of the importance of senior management involvement in outsourcing decisions (Figure 3.9 – see Chapter 2 on senior management involvement in the decision to outsource). In high-performing companies, most decisions to outsource are taken at executive committee level and by senior, business unit or functional level managers. In average-performing companies, a greater number of outsourcing decisions are taken at board level, which the Executive has then to implement. In high-performing companies, those managers directly accountable for outsourcing are given full responsibility for the taking and implementing of outsourcing decisions. The board are informed of the decisions and are kept abreast of progress. Managers are trusted to do their job!

Becoming outsource ready

Case study: negotiating HR outsourcing in an international bank

> *Managing Director*: Thank you so much for the proposal. I will put it forward to my colleagues on the Executive.

Box   *Continued*

Consultant:	What do you think the likely reaction will be to rethinking how HR (human resources) should be positioned in the Bank?
Managing Director:	I do not know. What I do know is that we really do need to consider how HR should be handled from now on! We do not need all the HR people we have got. The more transactional jobs and activities can be outsourced. The question is which jobs add value and how can we make HR more effective?
Consultant:	So you think that most of your colleagues would agree that HR needs looking at?
Managing Director:	Oh yes. The question is can they and the HR director cope with being examined? You see, I know that I want HR to be a key driver of change throughout the organisation. HR itself would welcome that. My board and executive committee colleagues would, in principle, agree. The question is, is the rest of the organisation prepared to have HR disassembled and put back together in a more meaningful way and also is the HR director ready for such scrutiny? Logic is one thing. Getting people to be ready for change is another!

The consultant in the case above had just submitted a proposal for outsourcing HR to the Managing Director (MD) of one of the key business units of a multi-national bank. The MD is viewed as a powerful figure in the senior team, influential in determining the bank's strategy. The MD's view is that the HR function requires fundamental scrutiny for two reasons. First, he considers that many posts in the human resources department are so transactionally oriented that they can be sourced out to a service provider, or the individuals made redundant, as technology can offer a more cost effective service. Second, those individuals and roles in the HR function that can provide a positive value adding contribution to the bank's strategic development should be enabled to do so. The MD's intention is to have key HR staff and managers working closely with senior line management and board members, so that HR can better facilitate the changes that need to be driven through the bank. Despite the MD's intention of working to better integrate HR with line management and the Board, he recognises that certain of his line and HR colleagues may not be prepared for the upheaval that follows a strategic audit and diagnosis and the subsequent outsourcing of transactional activities. He understands that outsourcing can only be effectively pursued when the organisation is 'outsource ready'.

The Kakabadse survey indicates that many companies recognise the importance of being outsource ready as a prelude to undertaking outsourcing. Becoming outsource ready requires attending to two issues, having determined the feasibility for outsourcing and whether the organisation is capable of appropriately resourcing the outsourcing strategies that need to be pursued. Being clear as to how feasible is the proposed programme of outsourcing involves,

- ascertaining whether clear agreement has been reached on which activities should be targeted for outsourcing;
- being realistic concerning the level of experience needed in the organisation for outsourcing;
- being realistic as to the risk management capabilities of the host organisation;
- appreciating the level of demand made on staff and management and the flexibility required to manage the transition and the disruption that results from outsourcing.

Resourcing a combination of outsourcing strategies requires that,

- the outsourcing strategies pursued support the company's key organisational strategies;
- sufficient consideration has been given to the resourcing requirement of all phases of each outsourcing initiative;
- sufficient attention and resources have been allocated to improving internal communications, particularly through staff briefings;
- line management are sufficiently prepared to deal with unforeseen contingencies.

Table 3.3 sets out the differences between high- and average-performing companies in terms of the feasibility for and resourcing of, outsourcing. The senior managers of high-performing companies rate their

Table 3.3 Being outsource ready

Capability	Company	
Outsource ready	High performing	Average performing
• Clear targeting	✓✓✓	✓✓✓
• Level of outsourcing experience	✓✓✓	✓✓
• Risk management capability	✓✓✓	✓✓
• Managing the transition	✓✓✓	✓
• Outsourcing strategy integrated with organisation strategy	✓✓✓	✓
• Resourcing all phases of outsourcing initiatives	✓✓	✓
• Staff briefings	✓✓	✓
• Contingency management	✓✓✓	✓

Note: ✓✓✓ – Well prepared; ✓✓ – Prepared; ✓ – Poorly prepared.

organisation as well prepared for resourcing and managing the various outsourcing strategies being pursued. How outsourcing contributes to the strategies pursued by the organisation is also clearly appreciated. It is recognised that staff briefings and the ability to resource all phases of the various outsource initiatives require special attention. As one senior manager commented, 'getting the resources and briefing staff are the two areas where you are always working to get it right but left with a feeling that you will never get there.'

The senior managers of average-performing companies rate themselves as well-prepared for clearly targeting what needs to be outsourced. In contrast, they consider themselves poorly prepared for managing their organisation through the transition of transferring resources to suppliers as a result of having embarked on one or more outsourcing programmes. Equally problematic is senior management's capability to integrate the programmes of outsourcing with the strategies being pursued by the organisation. Part of the reason for poorly integrating outsourcing strategy with organisation strategy is that insufficient attention is given to resourcing the various phases of the outsourcing programme. Another part is that, as discussed at the beginning of this chapter, the senior management of the organisation do not share the same view as to the value that can be gained from outsourcing (Figure 3.1). It is virtually impossible to integrate two sets of strategies when top management are not clear why they are committing themselves to particular programmes of outsourcing in the first place. Being unsure of the reason for undertaking outsourcing also affects the preparedness

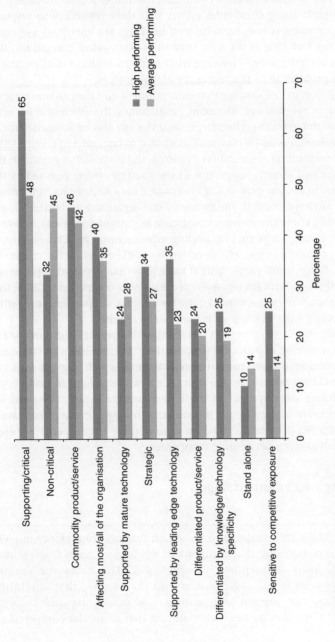

Figure 3.10 Status of outsourcing.
Note: Respondents selected multiple options.

and flexibility of management to respond to unexpected occurrences. This point is emphasised by the fact that the senior managers of average-performing companies report that their capability to respond to contingencies is low. Equally, staff briefings are identified as poorly conducted but that is an area that high-performing companies also indicate is challenging. Knowing what to do in terms of outsourcing is less of a problem than managing the actual process.

In addition to low management commitment and the inadequate level of resources invested in outsourcing programmes, the differences between the high- and average-performing companies can also be accounted for in terms of the status and importance attributed to outsourcing (Figure 3.10). In high-performing organisations, outsourcing is viewed as critical to the enterprise and directly supportive of the strategies being pursued by the company. In average-performing companies, outsourcing programmes are viewed as non-critical to the future of the organisation. Further, high-performing companies view outsourcing as commanding an important strategic status, supported by leading edge technology. Outsourcing is seen as providing a competitive advantage, differentiating the enterprise from its competitors, particularly if knowledge management applications emerge through outsourcing. Average-performing companies indicate that if programmes of outsourcing require technology support, mature rather than leading edge technology is likely to be required.

Overall, the survey results show that becoming outsource-ready requires investing resources to support the management of programmes of outsourcing and ensuring that outsourcing is well aligned with the strategies being pursued by the firm. The more important outsourcing is to the future development of the enterprise, the greater the need for alignment. The survey results indicate that high-performing companies have prepared themselves to be more responsive to competitive conditions than average-performing companies.

Pursuing concurrent strategies

Increasingly, companies are focusing on the core competence model and are recognising that competitive advantage comes from working the truly differentiated competences. This takes the senior management of the organisation into the mindset that anything that does not support differentiation is defocusing and is best executed by other parties who major on that particular competence

> or activity. An example would be in the energy market where... customer service and the identification of key segments is important. The actual management of those circumstances within segments is seen very much as a matter of process and behaviour, best done by those who specifically do this for a number of parties – Tom Drury, CEO, Vertex

Tom Drury draws attention to a crucial consideration for senior management. Identify the core competences of the organisation in order to position the firm to sustain competitive advantage. As argued in Chapter 2, market life cycles have become increasingly shorter, partly because markets are maturing and partly because of information systems technology. Firms experience fewer growth opportunities and greater competition for market share. Further, it is generally agreed that sustainable top class performance will not occur if there is misalignment between a firm's competitive strategy and market requirements. The question remains, what is core and what is non-core to the enterprise in ever-changing market conditions?

> Well that's a key issue. What is core. What is not core. That's always the debate. We would say that the actual steel making itself and the marketing of our steel we would see as core and activities around that we would see as non-core. But these things are arbitrary ... we have people who say we will lubricate your whole mill ... we'll give you the whole service. Basically, what's core and critical keep changing. Tomorrow, I may see things differently – Top Manager, International Steel Manufacturer

As discussed in Chapter 2, despite the emphasis in the literature as to whether the core competences of the company are more of a concern of economy of scale or knowledge management considerations, the Kakabadse survey results clearly show that companies pursue a number of outsourcing strategies simultaneously as the nature of gaining competitive advantage itself changes.

Attempting to achieve multiple objectives through outsourcing applies to high-performing as well as the average-performing companies (Figure 3.11). High-performing companies, in particular, pursue a mix of outsourcing strategies which are more knowledge driven than cost-based. The two predominant sourcing strategies adopted by high-performing

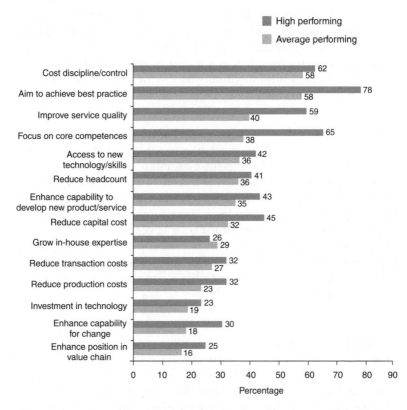

Figure 3.11   Concurrent sourcing strategies.
Note: Respondents selected multiple options.

companies are concerned with aiming to achieve best practice and focusing on the core competences of the organisation to achieve sustainable competitive advantage. Improving service quality and applying cost disciplines and controls follow close behind.

Further, strategies which reduce headcount and capital costs are as popular as gaining access to new technology and skills and enhancing the capability of the organisation to develop new products and services. As the steel company manager observes, what is viewed as core to the organisation changes with new market challenges. A different combination of processes and activities may be sourced in or sourced out according to the particular demands of customers and the supply chain. For average-performing companies, aiming to achieve best practice and being disciplined over the management of costs stand out. After that no

Table 3.4 Integrating ways of working: high vs. average performing companies

Capability	Company	
Integrative skills	**High performing**	**Average performing**
• Rearrange ways of working	✓✓	–
• Integrate around activities already outsourced	✓✓✓	✓
• Benchmark against quality standard	✓✓✓	✓
• Value added through outsourcing	✓✓	✓
• Apply quality controls	✓✓✓	✓

Note: ✓✓✓ – well prepared; ✓✓ – prepared; ✓ – poorly prepared.

particular combination of outsourcing strategies is favoured. Undertaking outsourcing for improving service quality or leveraging the core competences of the organisation, is not as prominent in average-performing companies.

High-performing companies report that the reason a varying combination of outsourcing strategies is pursued is to improve the position of the organisation in the 'value chain'. The survey highlights that, in order to move up the value chain, the management of the organisation need to learn how to integrate different ways of working as a result of pursuing strategies that do not 'fit well' together. Further, to maintain the momentum of change, management need to agree on the value that has been gained through outsourcing. Integrating contrasting ways of operating involves,

• helping staff and management to change the way they work as a result of outsourcing;
• introducing disciplines which enable integration with service providers around activities already outsourced;
• being able to improve performance against known quality standards;
• agreeing at senior management levels that value added has been gained through outsourcing;
• being disciplined to regularly apply quality controls.

Table 3.4 sets out the differences in capability to integrate different ways of working between high- and average-performing companies.

Managing the staff and the middle level management of the organisation to adopt new ways of working as a result of outsourcing is
reported as a strenuous and demanding experience for both high- and
average-performing companies. High-performing companies report
higher levels of capability and preparedness in this arena. A telling
difference between high- and average-performing companies lies in the
area of being able to well integrate with suppliers to whom activities
have already been outsourced. High-performing companies enjoy more
positive relationships with their suppliers, so that changes in agreement, or accommodating contingencies that arise, are managed with
only minimal disruption to current arrangements. High-performing companies also benchmark performance against agreed quality standards
and apply appropriate quality controls to ensure that standards are
maintained. Average-performing companies indicate that they have
a poor track record in integrating with suppliers who already provide
them with outsourcing services, benchmarking against known quality
standards and applying quality controls.

One reason why the management of high-performing companies
maintain discipline in pulling together different outsourcing strategies
is that they regularly review the progress being achieved. The senior
management of both high- and average-performing companies report
that reaching agreement on the progress that has been gained through
outsourcing is challenging. In large, more complex organisations,
different activities and subsidiaries are likely to be at different points in
their economic life cycle. Value is likely to hold different meaning for
the managers of the various parts of the corporation. Hence a corporate
view on how to move forward and on progress being made is difficult to
achieve. The senior managers of high-performing companies report that
they are better prepared to enter into the value adding debate owing to
the effort they have made to become a more effective top team. Lack of
attention to team leadership in average-performing companies is
reflected in their difficulties in being both strategically and operationally
effective.

Managing details

Case study: Clare Spottiswoode, former gas industry regulator

Interviewer:	... what is required for properly managing a sourcing relationship?

Clare Spottiswoode:	Clearly understanding what you want. So writing a very clear contract, a very clear service agreement that says exactly what you want and then continue monitoring that. In our case, our industry was very much part of that. We had to continuously check that we were performing, not just by statistics, but by ringing up with all sorts of problems and finding out what's going on and, of course, taking up any complaints that we got ... It really was a very successful operation.

Clare Spottiswoode, as well as being the former gas industry regulator, has also been a consultant with PA Consulting Group and is currently chairperson of Bill Buster, Newco and joint chair of Utility.com. She places substantial emphasis on the clarity of contract between service purchaser and service provider and the monitoring of such agreements. In fact, for her, clarity of agreement needs to be matched by being 'hands on' and responsive to solving problems and not just relying on trends and statistics. The point Clare Spottiswoode is making is, know what is happening around you and pay attention to detail.

Such views are strongly echoed by the Kakabadse survey participants. Managing outsourcing contracts requires demonstrable capability in,

- having proven processes in place for selecting service providers;
- developing a capacity in the organisation to manage a variety of outsourcing arrangements;
- benchmarking service level agreements;
- monitoring performance against agreed service levels;
- developing a discipline in the organisation for the transfer of resources and assets;
- learning from previous experiences of managing a variety of outsourcing arrangements.

As well as the Spottiswoode requirements for clear service level agreements and monitoring performance against these agreements, the survey results show that managing outsourcing arrangements also requires instituting processes for selecting appropriate service providers and for being able to manage the transfer of resources from service purchaser to service provider. To build up an expertise in the organisation for managing outsourcing, the learning from previous experiences needs to be captured. Table 3.5 displays the differences between high- and average-performing companies in terms of managing the daily transactional elements of outsourcing.

High-performing companies display greater capability in developing processes for the selection of service providers. They also report greater versatility in drafting and administering a variety of outsourcing arrangements, and more effective monitoring of performance against service level agreements. They further report an expertise in transferring resources to service providers. High-performing companies display that they have made the effort to capture the learning from previous experiences of outsourcing. Average-performing companies struggle in these areas except for having developed a discipline of learning from previous outsourcing initiatives. However, it is questionable whether such learning is being applied. Two areas which both high- and average-performing companies find demanding are developing the expertise for the effective transfer of resources to the service provider and appropriately benchmarking service level agreements. The reason benchmarking is problematic for both high- and average-performing companies is that the host organisation and service provider are driven by different service level expectations.

As with becoming outsource ready, the difference between high- and average-performing organisations lies not in recognising of what needs to be done to ensure high quality sourcing but in managing the process itself.

Table 3.5   Managing outsourcing: high vs. average performing companies

Capability	Company	
Managing outsourcing	High performing	Average performing
• Selecting service providers	✓✓✓	✓
• Managing varying outsource arrangements	✓✓✓	✓
• Benchmarking service level agreements	✓	✓
• Monitoring performance against service level agreements	✓✓✓	✓
• Managing the transfer of resources	✓✓	✓
• Capturing previous outsourcing experiences	✓✓✓	✓✓

Note: ✓✓✓ – Well prepared; ✓✓ – Prepared; ✓ – Poorly prepared.

Promoting quality relationships

Interviewer:	Is there a shortage in the market of skilled people who can manage relationships with outsourcing suppliers?
Jim Leng:	I know it is difficult to judge whether this is a national characteristic . . . but there is a shortage. Probably what's happening is that standards are getting higher and what was acceptable yesterday is not acceptable today – Jim Leng, CEO, Laporte plc

Jim Leng recognises the importance of developing high quality relationships in establishing satisfactory outsourcing arrangements. However, he feels that the skills required for effective relationship management are progressing at a pace faster than companies are able to train their staff and managers.

The Kakabadse survey results support the Jim Leng view of the need to develop the skills for high quality relationships between service purchasers and service providers. The skills required for effectively managing supplier relationships are identified as,

- the ability to develop a shared understanding between partners;
- the ability to recognise the level of cultural match between partners;
- the skills to foster high quality relations;
- the ability to manage relationships through changes in contractual obligations;
- the skills to manage consortium-based relationships.

The survey also shows that, to promote high quality supplier/customer relationships, attention needs to be paid to managing the relationships within the host organisation. Other important factors are,

- motivating staff;
- motivating lower and middle level management;
- enabling employees to improve their performance.

Tables 3.6 and 3.7 highlight the differences between high- and average-performing companies in the terms of the attention given to managing supplier relationships and motivating staff and management within the host organisation.

Table 3.6 Managing supplier relations: high vs. average performing companies

Capability	Company	
Supplier relations	High performing	Average performing
• Shared understanding between partners	✓✓✓	✓✓✓
• Cultural match between partners	✓✓✓	✓
• Relationship management skills	✓✓✓	✓
• Managing changes in contractual obligations	✓✓✓	✓✓
• Consortium management skills	✓✓	✓✓

Note: ✓✓✓ – Well prepared; ✓✓ – Prepared; ✓ – Poorly prepared.

Table 3.6 displays the performance similarities and differences between high- and average-performing companies concerning the capability to manage supplier relationships. Developing a shared understanding between partners and having the skills to manage consortium type relationships are reported as comparable and well developed. Three areas, however, are identified as showing differences in levels of performance. High-performing companies report that, first, they are better prepared to assess the level of cultural match between prospective partners and, second, they more efficiently manage changes that arise with existing contractual obligations, than do average-performing firms. Third, the area with the greatest degree of difference is relationship management skills. Average-performing companies are ill prepared to sustain a positive relationship between themselves and their suppliers. Less consideration is given in average-performing companies to improve the people skills of their staff and management.

Table 3.7 Managing internal relations: high vs. average performing companies

Capability	Company	
Staff motivation and performance	High performing	Average performing
• Motivating staff	✓✓✓	✓
• Motivating management	✓✓✓	✓✓
• Improving employee performance levels	✓✓✓	✓

Note: ✓✓✓ – Well prepared; ✓✓ – Prepared; ✓ – Poorly prepared.

The greatest difference in terms of relationship management skills is in the area of motivating staff, which is shown to require substantial attention in average-performing companies (Table 3.7). A similar trend is captured in Table 3.4 which indicates that staff briefings are particularly weak in average-performing companies. Moreover, the capability to motivate lower- and middle-level management and the managerial skills to improve the levels of employee performance are reported as not as well developed in average-performing, as compared to high-performing companies.

The differences in the quality of service purchaser/service provider relationships and in the skills of managing supplier relationships, are more evident when examining the overall quality of sourcing relationships, as reported by high- and average-performing companies (Figure 3.12). Being more cooperative and more open and transparent with external suppliers is more evident with high-performing companies, and building partnership-based relationships is given greater priority in high-performing companies. Average-performing companies report that they concentrate more on the contractual elements of the service purchaser/service provider relationship. The differences between high-performing and average-performing companies in the areas of flexibly responding to clients and showing respect to partners and suppliers, are not as great as on the other factors above.

The performance variance between high- and average-performing companies lies in the level of skills to manage the relationship between the host organisation and service providers, but not in the type of service providers chosen (Figure 3.13). Similar types of service providers are

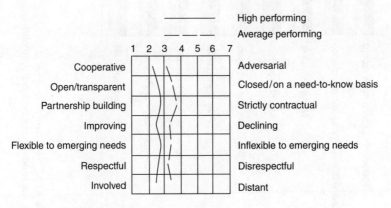

Figure 3.12 Quality of sourcing relationship(s).

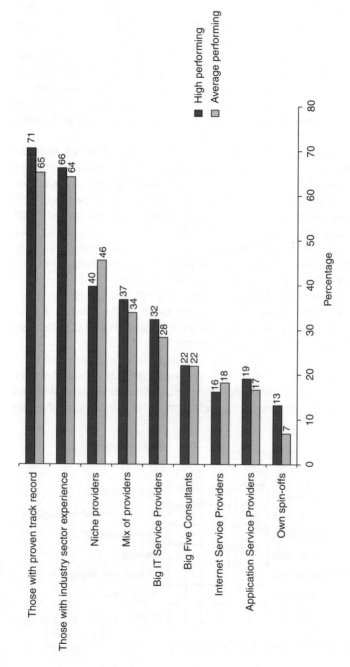

Figure 3.13 Preferred service providers.
Note: Respondents selected multiple options.

preferred by both high- and average-performing companies. High-performing companies marginally prefer to work with service providers who have a proven track record within one or more areas of specialism, whilst average-performing companies report a greater preference for niche providers.

However, differences in capability between high- and average-performing companies, particularly in terms of investing sufficient resources to outsourcing programmes, benchmarking quality standards, monitoring service level agreements, aligning the outsourcing strategy with organisation strategy and being flexible in response to contractual changes, are reported as strongly determining the choice of outsourcing arrangements (Figure 3.14). Average-performing companies more readily enter into single contracts with preferred and trusted suppliers. Such arrangements are deemed safer. High-performing companies tend to be more flexible in their sourcing arrangements, preferring performance-based contracts, strategic alliances and various partnership or other relationship arrangements with multiple suppliers. High-performing companies also adopt traditional single contracts with preferred suppliers. The repertoire of capabilities to manage a variety of outsourcing contracts and to select appropriate providers is evident amongst high-performing companies. As Figure 3.13 shows, it is not the type of provider that is the crucial issue, but the choice of which supplier is best suited to the contract in question.

Impact

When we examine the impact of outsourcing on the host organisation, the differences between high- and average-performing companies, particularly concerning the degree of commitment at senior levels to outsourcing and the levels of capability for the managing of outsourcing initiatives and different outsourcing arrangements, are noticeable (Figure 3.15).

The greatest advantage of outsourcing, in both high- and average-performing companies, is the sharpening of focus on the core competences of the organisation. By being more disciplined in leveraging the key strengths of the organisation, high-performing companies report greater cost savings, greater improvements in service quality, enhanced operational flexibility, greater efficiency gains, a more motivated management and more effective use of in-house staff, than do average-performing companies. Largely because of the staff reductions and redundancies that are reported to arise from outsourcing, poor staff motivation remains an issue for both high- and average-performing companies. As a result of improved levels of organisational performance, high-performing

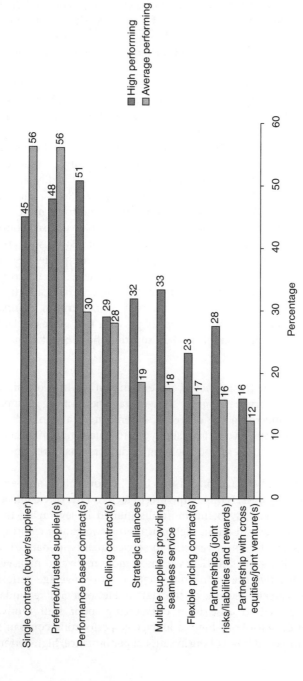

Figure 3.14 Nature of sourcing arrangements.
Note: Respondents selected multiple options.

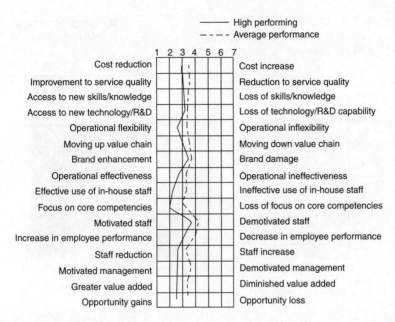

Figure 3.15 Impact of outsourcing.

companies report that they are able to exploit a greater number of value adding opportunities.

With such improvements in performance, high-performing companies report higher levels of satisfaction with outsourcing. A more varied response emerges over the levels of satisfaction with outsourcing for average-performing organisations (Figure 3.16). Average-performing companies report far more mixed results concerning the impact of, and satisfaction with, outsourcing than do high-performing companies.

Summary

- Sixty-nine companies display the capabilities for best practice outsourcing.
- The key distinguishing feature between high- and average-performing companies, which influences all other outsourcing performance characteristics, is the degree of shared view at senior management levels as to the value to be gained from outsourcing. Analysis of organisation size, age of managers, regional location and the power to purchase outsourcing services shows a similar profile between high- and average-performing companies.

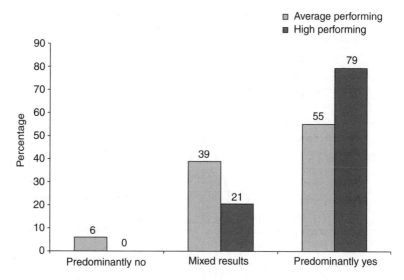

Figure 3.16   Satisfaction with outsourcing.

- Five-core capabilities emerge for managing outsourcing contracts and arrangements. They are: trusting the managers in the organisation to undertake the outsourcing programmes they consider necessary, preparing the organisation to become outsource ready, developing the skills to integrate and align concurrently pursued strategies of outsourcing, developing the operational skills to manage the details of outsourcing contracts and nurturing high quality relationships with suppliers and other stakeholder organisations.
- In high-performing companies, the decisions to outsource and the accountability for the management of outsourcing arrangements are located at executive committee and at general management levels. In average-performing companies, a greater proportion of outsourcing decisions and the accountability for outsourcing contracts are located at board level.
- Both high- and average-performing companies concurrently pursue a mix of outsourcing strategies.
- Becoming outsource ready requires analysing both the feasibility of outsourcing and the resourcing implications of simultaneously pursuing a number of outsourcing strategies.
- Pursuing concurrent outsourcing strategies requires management to have the capabilities to integrate contrasting ways of working. To

motivate line management to continue to attend to issues of alignment between differing sourcing strategies, senior management need to agree, and communicate to the rest of the organisation, the value that is being gained from outsourcing.

- Managing outsourcing contracts requires attention to the appropriate selection of service providers, benchmarking service level agreements and consistently monitoring performance against those agreements, effectively transferring resources from the host organisation to the service provider and capturing the learning from previous outsourcing experiences.
- Promoting positive relationships between the host organisation and suppliers requires responding to the different needs that arise between service purchasers and service providers and managing any subsequent changes to contractual agreements. Also important is motivating the staff and management in the host organisation to be flexible to meet new needs.
- The difference in levels of outsourcing preparedness and capability between high- and average-performing companies is reflected in the quality of sourcing relationships between the host organisation and service providers. High-performing companies have developed more positive relationships with their suppliers. Little variation exists between high- and average-performing companies concerning the types of service providers preferred.
- The difference in outsourcing preparedness and capability between high- and average-performing companies is reflected in the outcomes that emerge from outsourcing. High-performing companies report greater levels of operational flexibility and operational effectiveness, a greater focus on core competences, more motivated management, greater value added achieved and greater opportunity gains from outsourcing, than average-performing companies.
- High-performing companies are more likely to enter into performance-based contracts and strategic alliances and partnerships which share risks and rewards, whereas average-performing companies are more likely to negotiate single contracts with preferred and trusted suppliers.
- High-performing companies report higher levels of satisfaction with outsourcing than average-performing organisations.

References and further reading

For further information on discretionary leadership, read Jaques (1951; 1979) and Kakabadse and Kakabadse (1999). For how top teams function, read Kakabadse

(2000), Kakabadse (2001), Kay (1993), Kim and Mauborgne (1997), and Pricewater-houseCoopers (1999).

For further information on the Cranfield studies, read Kakabadse (1991), Kakabadse and Myers (1996) and Kakabadse et al. (1996).

For further reading on the competences required for outsourcing and latest trends in best practice outsourcing, read Kakabadse and Kakabadse (2000a; 2000b), Christian (1997), Davidow and Malone (1992), Hupfeld (1997), Lacity, Willcocks and Feeny (1995), Mahe and Perras (1994), Narin (1999), Teng, Cheon and Grover (1995) and Willcocks, Fitzgerald and Feeny (1995).

4
Looking Ahead

Case studies – the future of sourcing

> ...whatever is your source of competitive advantage! What is it that you do that other people cannot do and perhaps that is where companies struggle...We are thinking very hard about that question... On the power station side, moving power stations isn't important – operating them more competitively than anyone else is important. I think the ability to buy and sell energy is very important...Knowing how to do it is the core,...You are left with relatively few areas of knowledge based activity rather than asset based activity that you want to keep within your direct control – Graham Brown, National Power

> ...I don't believe we will outsource anything else of major significance in the next few years...We need to improve the management of our current suppliers properly, getting the best value from them and that will not happen overnight...Huge disadvantages if we fail! For example, do you know how much effort it takes to change suppliers? The workload is incredible and more importantly, the operational risk is high...For us, we can now tap into all sorts of expertise, not just the primary supplier. That's the way I see outsourcing companies going. They can realise more innovation and share risk, by going into joint venture partnerships – Linda Shaw, British Airways

> ...I think ultimately we will have to devise a way of how we develop technology, how we develop software, what really is the efficient way, what does the bank require. Almost every bank I've dealt with has essentially appallingly bad architecture and most of them have the old legacy system. The competitive pressures will be: you've either got to have a very efficient end-to-end processes or at some point you get overtaken ... I think outsourcing will get us through to a point and insourcing skills will get us through to a point, but eventually you're going to stop being able to cut the component costs and say, we do actually need 000's of people – Michael McGrath, Deutsche Bank

Three contrasting views are expressed concerning the future for outsourcing by managers well versed in the science of positioning and repositioning infrastructure for the benefit of the enterprise. Graham Brown, Chief Operating Officer, National Power, views that focusing on the core competences of the company will determine the nature of future and practice of outsourcing.

Linda Shaw, General Manager, Contracts Management – Procurement, British Airways, offers a contrasting view for the future of outsourcing. She considers that greater attention needs to be given to the service purchaser/service provider relationship. Being innovative in outsourcing means improving the service arrangements between the two parties, but not in changing suppliers.

Different again is Michael McGrath, Director, Deutsche Bank, who considers the use of technology as an important consideration to future outsourcing arrangements. Michael McGrath and Graham Brown share one perspective as both consider that attending to the core requirements of the enterprise will seriously influence the nature of future outsourcing contracts and types of relationships.

The picture that is being painted by the three senior managers is, recognise what is both core and critical to the business and source (outsource or insource) accordingly. These three managers reflect the sentiments and views expressed by academic and business writers alike concerning servicing future sourcing requirements. Following an exploration of likely future outsourcing practice as discussed in the literature, this chapter examines the results of the Kakabadse survey on future outsourcing trends. Although considerable similarity is identified with current practice, it is shown that managing a greater number of supplier relationships in a more sensitive and sophisticated manner is likely in the future. We conclude that to enhance the organisation's capability to manage ever more intricate supplier relations, a 'keiretsu mindset' will be a necessary requirement for the future.

Paradigm shift

As outlined in Chapter 2, throughout the 1990s the business press and academic literature were peppered with the argument that managers need to readjust from managing vertically integrated organisations to nurturing a portfolio of contractual relationships. The shift that has taken place in organisations has been from attention to size, specialisation and well-structured job descriptions, to speed, quality of service and integration through the supply chain, all to achieve greater value and flexibility so as to enable the enterprise to be more competitive. A number of writers agree that such efforts have achieved quantifiable and visible results in terms of enhanced supply chain management, more effective management of the costs in the organisation and better service standards.

Within a likely business context of needing to manage extended horizontal relationships, six key drivers determining the future viability and practice of outsourcing are identified in the literature (Table 4.1), namely:

1 the future strategic drivers for outsourcing;
2 the nature of the future outsourcing market;
3 changes in organisational structure;
4 the nature of the future client/supplier interface;
5 the impact of IT;
6 developments in performance management.

The view being portrayed is that the economic climate is rapidly changing. The need for greater advantage cost and access-to-market synergies has spawned a wave of mergers and acquisitions. Shareholders demand more effective capital utilisation in the context of growing IT usage. More oligopolistic organisations are likely to be formed, but innovative, 'fast of foot' new entrants are also likely to emerge. Hence, enterprises of varying sizes have had to, and will have to reconsider how to confront changing environmental pressures and yet remain competitive in a demanding and volatile market place. The trends from the literature captured in Table 4.1 display that enterprises will continue to reposition themselves so as to attempt to move higher up on the value chain and

Table 4.1 Outsourcing paradigm shift

Elements	Previous outsourcing paradigm	New outsourcing paradigm
1. Strategic drivers Drivers	• Reduction/control of operating costs • Availability of capital funds • Cash infusion • Specialisation • Access to expert skills • Emphasis on functions	• Grow and stay competitive (e.g. lower cost and improve services) • Global competition • Focus on core competences – redirect internal skills/capabilities and resources to high value-added areas • Improved business focus • Move to flatter organisation • Search for greater flexibility • Customer value • Shared risk
What is being outsourced Decision based on	Non-core functions • Strategic vs. commodity approach • Single function • Efficiency gains	Business processes/intellectual capital • Value creation • Whole process (e.g. greater shareholder value across the enterprise) • Efficiency and effectiveness gains.
2. Market Outsourcing market	• Large corporations • Manufacturing	• Large scale businesses • Medium and small businesses • Government • Outsourcing vendors • Service and manufacturing

Growth market	• Predominantly USA, UK and Australia • 1997 ($90 bn)	• Global and sectoral (e.g. retail, financial services) • 2002 ($120 bn) • Public services • Europe/Asia • Start ups
3. Organisational structure Effects of outsourcing	'Hollow Organisation' (empty box/organisation)	'Virtual Organisation' interconnected relationships
Outsourcing arrangements	• Take over of existing assets • Up-front payment from the supplier to client for the client's IT assets • Performance improvement and cost reduction in the clients' IT operations	• Suppliers install and run new systems • Unit cost reduction • Savings go into R&D and systems innovation • Savings and profits shared with vendors
Organisational shape	• Vertical integration • Diversified corporation	• Networked organisation • Specialised corporation
4. Supplier interface Supplier choice	• Single supplier offering one-size-fits-all • Entire IT operation handed over to one big supplier	• Multiple suppliers or 'Best-of-breed' approach • Different suppliers are selected for each area of specialisation • Expected to provide seamless service • Industry sector driven (e.g. Shared Service Centres)
Provider specialisation Contracts	Technology, and business driven • With individual suppliers • Purchaser/Supplier	• Individual suppliers • Consortia of suppliers • Joint ventures, shared risk, equity stakes, consortia, spin-offs, partnerships
Duration	Variable, depending on activity, between 3 and 7 years	Variable but generally longer, often 10 to 15 years

Table 4.1 (continued)

Elements	Previous outsourcing paradigm	New outsourcing paradigm
Service providers	Hardware suppliers and consultancies	Software/hardware suppliers, consortia of suppliers, niche spin-offs, consultancies
5. Information technology		
IT outsourcing	Maintenance, hardware/network, application development of IT Systems	• Business process management (BPM) • Software as Service (ASPs) • Applications and website hosting • E-business facilities
IT/Business processing delineation	Clear difference	Arbitrary delineation (i.e. e-commerce redefines trading)
Outsourcing differentiation	Information systems *vs.* Business processes	Business processes (e.g. core *vs.* non-core). Buy or rent decisions
Cost of data storage	Complex costing (including storage medium, file size, frequency of access, etc.)	Cost-per-megabyte/per month basis as other utilities (e.g. electricity, gas)
Network	Primary vehicle for service delivery	Primary trading medium (e.g. e-business)
Desktop function	Productive tool	Main interface with employees, suppliers and customers (e.g. e-commerce, Intranets)
6. Performance management		
Management focus	Enhancing vertically integrated configuration	Managing portfolio of relationships
Communication focus on	Control of activities	Complex coordination
Primary skills	Monitoring performance (e.g. procurement and contract management)	Managing relationships and/or 'virtual corporation'

Flexibility	Limited, additional services based on agreed schedule of rates	• Flexibility based on rapid and full sharing of information • Adjustments are negotiated for scale or scope
Scalability	Slow	Fast
Control	Detailed performance provisions, including monitoring, penalties and guarantees	Cooperation, monitoring, sharing of benefits and risks
Recontracting	Primarily to renegotiate terms of contract and/or change supplier	Primarily to reposition and reinvigorate the relationship with the supplier
Dispute resolution	• Mechanisms stated in contract including the provision for specific arbitration • Legal processes	• Expectation is that potential disputes are resolved before they reach adversarial level • Emphasis on risk management and conflict resolution • No formal mechanisms specified • Legal processes as last resort
Success dependent on	Choice of the supplier	Preparation and the commitment to manage outsourcing

Source: Compiled from Kakabadse and Kakabadse (2000b).

thus, gain competitive advantage. To enable such mobility, the view projected is that corporations will restructure on the basis of horizontal, partnership-based, contractual arrangements. Fundamental to achieving competitive advantage will be the identifying and strengthening of the core competences of the enterprise. Part of the process of core competence enhancement will be to attend more to the disciplined management of costs and the improving of efficiency through a variety of arrangements. Various academic and business writers indicate that to continue to be successful, strong and viable, relationships with a chain of suppliers in order to improve levels of quality at justifiable costs, will be imperative. In effect, current trends are likely to continue into the future.

The Kakabadse survey

The survey explores four key aspects of future outsourcing:

1 the reasons for future outsourcing;
2 the nature of future outsourcing arrangements, including how such arrangements are likely to affect the employment prospects of employees;
3 the processes, activities and functions targeted for outsourcing;
4 the 'keiretsu-like-nature' of the competences necessary for effectively realising the benefits to be gained from outsourcing.

Future outsourcing reasons

The survey results indicate that the key reason for undertaking outsourcing in the future will be for the host organisation to achieve best practice in whatever area, a process or activity is targeted (Figure 4.1). From thereon in, two clusters of reasons for future outsourcing also emerge as important. In support of achieving best practice, the first cluster of reasons links the adoption of new technology through best-in-class suppliers whilst maintaining strict control over costs.

The second cluster of reasons concentrate around the enhancement of capability within the organisation. Specifically, improvements in service quality, a continued focus on core competences and the strengthening of the firm's product/service portfolio, are the areas seen as important for improving the organisations' capability to compete. As with the current reasons for outsourcing (see Chapter 2), reducing costs through various means is likely to continue into the future. In comparison to the current outsourcing trends discussed in Chapter 2, the one difference to emerge

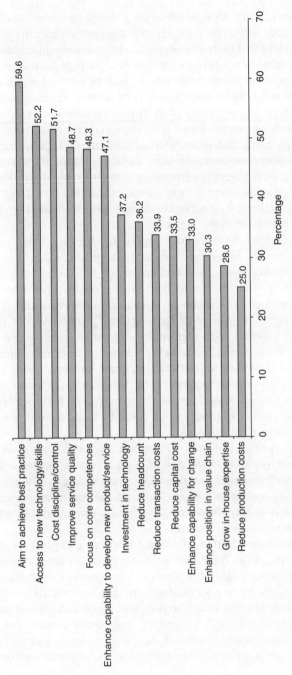

Figure 4.1 Future outsourcing reasons.
Note: Respondents selected multiple options.

is that greater priority is predicted to be given to the sourcing of new technology and skills, to attain greater competitive advantage. Few respondents identified that outsourcing in the future would enable their organisation to be better prepared to pursue a strategy for mergers and acquisitions (not reported). And only a small number of respondents identified that spinning off the non-core parts of their organisation would enhance the level of profitability of the host organisation (not reported).

Similar trends concerning future outsourcing emerge when comparing the reasons given by the senior managers of the 69 high-performing companies against those managers from average-performing firms (Figure 4.2). Both high- and average-performing companies highlight that the advantage they expect to gain from outsourcing in the future will be to achieve best practice and equally have management maintain high levels of discipline over costs in the organisation.

Also, high-performing companies report that they are likely to give greater attention to accessing new technology and skills than will average-performing firms. Senior managers of high-performing firms report that they will attempt to gain greater competitive advantage through greater focus on the core competences of the organisation than will the managers of average-performing firms. Similar to the trends described in Chapter 3, high-performing companies indicate that they will continue to concentrate on reducing transaction costs and enhancing management's capability to lead through change in order to improve the company's position in the value chain. Although not reported, owing to the low-level of responses, few of the managers of high-performing companies believed that greater value could be realised from spinning off non-core parts of the business.

The trends captured in Figure 4.2 support the views propounded by Graham Brown, National Power and Michael McGrath, Deutsche Bank, namely that well managed programmes of outsourcing can help senior management to concentrate more clearly on the core competencies of the organisation and that greater competitive advantage can be gained through investments in technology.

International comparison of US, UK and European companies confirms that outsourcing in the future will probably be undertaken in order to achieve best practice (Figure 4.3). European companies express the view that gaining access to new technology through outsourcing will be of greater advantage to them than that displayed by US and UK companies. Further, European companies consider that future outsourcing will improve the cost-discipline skills of staff and managers and also concentrate more on management gaining greater competitive advantage

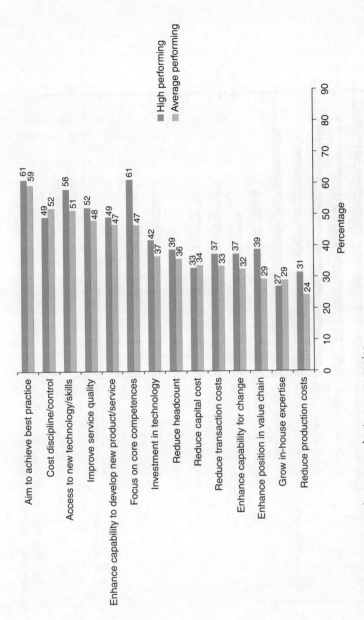

Figure 4.2 Future outsourcing reasons: best run companies.
Note: Respondents selected multiple options.

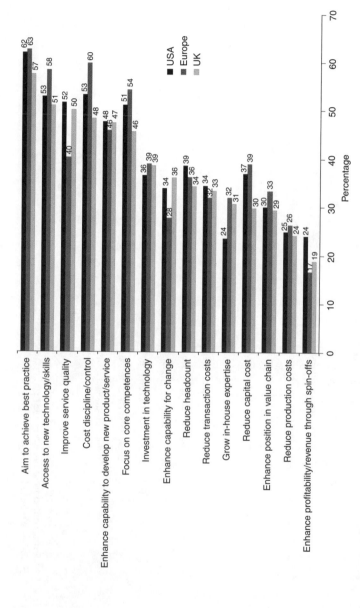

USA
Europe
UK

Aim to achieve best practice — 62, 63, 57
Access to new technology/skills — 53, 58, 51
Improve service quality — 52, 50, 40
Cost discipline/control — 53, 60, 48
Enhance capability to develop new product/service — 46, 48, 47
Focus on core competences — 51, 54, 46
Investment in technology — 36, 39, 39
Enhance capability for change — 34, 36, 28
Reduce headcount — 39, 36, 34
Reduce transaction costs — 34, 33, 32
Grow in-house expertise — 24, 32, 31
Reduce capital cost — 37, 39, 30
Enhance position in value chain — 30, 33, 29
Reduce production costs — 25, 26, 24
Enhance profitability/revenue through spin-offs — 24, 17, 19

Percentage

Figure 4.3 Future outsourcing reasons: international comparison.
Note: Respondents selected multiple options.

through better leveraging of the core competences of the organisation. In contrast, US and UK managers emphasise that in the future they will pay greater attention to improving service quality, enhancing their capability to drive through change and reducing headcount through the outsourcing programmes they will commission. Also, European and UK companies indicate that they are more likely to go the insourcing route by growing in-house expertise, whereas US companies report they more desire to 'spin-off' activities as stand-alone enterprises. Investment in technology as a mechanism for promoting greater efficiency and reducing the costs of transactional processes, is rated relatively equal on the list of future sourcing priorities by US, UK and European companies.

Future outsourcing arrangements

In keeping with the present-day trends discussed in Chapter 2, the most likely outsourcing relationship that will be contracted by service purchasers will be with preferred and trusted suppliers (Figure 4.4). This finding supports Linda Shaw of British Airways view, that once an organisation has developed positive relationships with supplier(s), the best sourcing strategy is to nurture and support such relationships but not to change suppliers. However, in contrast to the results presented in Chapter 2, greater attention is reported to be given in the future to performance-based contracts and partnership arrangements which involve joint risks, liabilities and rewards. Single contracts between service purchasers and providers are unlikely to enjoy as high a priority in the future as they do now. Outsourcing through strategic alliances or with multiple suppliers is considered to remain at a similar level of utilisation to today (see Chapter 2). A small number of respondents display their future preference for adopting shared service consortia arrangements. Further, certain public service organisations indicate their preference for adopting public/private finance initiatives (PFIs). As few respondents identified shared service consortia and PFIs as desired future outsourcing arrangements, these results are not included in Figure 4.4.

The differences of response from managers of high-performing companies as opposed to managers of average-performing companies, show that it is average-performing enterprises that display a greater preference for maintaining relationships with trusted suppliers, whilst high-performing companies will more prefer performance-based contracts (Figure 4.5). Equally, high-performing companies will pursue more strategic alliances and relationships with multiple suppliers in order to achieve the levels of service they desire, than will the average-performing enterprise. In contrast to the generic trends presented in Figure 4.4, high-performing

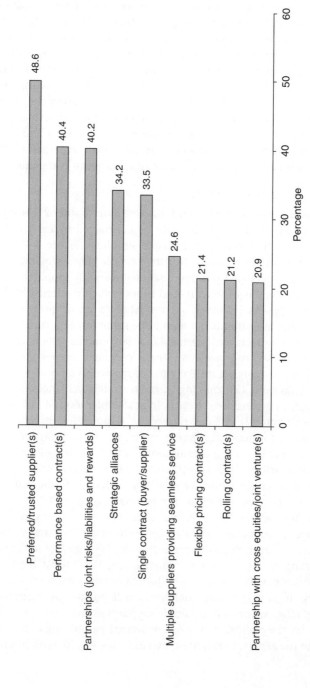

Figure 4.4 Future outsourcing arrangements.
Note: Respondents selected multiple options.

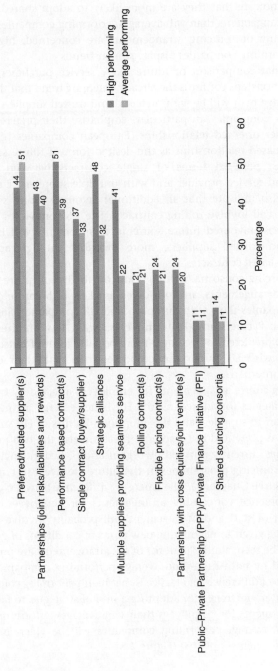

Figure 4.5 Future outsourcing arrangements: best run companies.
Note: Respondents selected multiple options.

companies indicate that they are more likely to adopt shared service consortia arrangements than will average-performing companies. As far as other future outsourcing arrangements are concerned, high- and average-performing companies display similar trends.

International comparison of future likely service purchaser/service provider relationships confirms the already emerging trend that the most popular arrangement will be with preferred and trusted suppliers (Figure 4.6). The UK companies, in particular, emphasise their preference for single supplier oriented relationships. European companies highlight partnership-based relationships as the desired form of future sourcing arrangements, both in terms of single contracts between service purchaser and service provider and with multiple suppliers. European companies also indicate that an additional favoured future sourcing arrangement will involve rolling contracts. The US companies predict that their most favoured future sourcing arrangements will be with preferred and trusted suppliers, more probably through adopting performance-based contracts.

Shared sourcing consortia, although low on the list of future desired outsourcing arrangements, are considered as likely to be more popular with US companies than with European and UK companies. Similarly, Private–Public Partnerships (PPP) and PFIs, again low on the list of priorities, are predicted to become a more popular form of outsourcing relationships with UK public service bodies than with their US and European counterparts.

Concerning future arrangements for employees affected by outsourcing, two strategies for addressing the HR issues emerge, namely, the transfer of staff to suppliers and the adoption of a mix of HR strategies (Figure 4.7). As presented in Chapter 2, these are also the two predominant strategies currently pursued by organisations. Redundancies arising from outsourcing programmes in the future are likely to remain at present levels (see Chapter 2). The emerging difference between current and future practice concerning arrangements for employees is that redeployment of staff and management will probably involve greater attention being given to negotiating new terms of conditions of employment. As can be seen, similar patterns of HR arrangements are predicted to be adopted by both high- and average-performing companies. The only two areas of differences of practice is that high-performing companies display a greater preference for adopting a mix of strategies to facilitate future arrangements for employees than will average-performing companies, whilst average-performing companies will be given more to transfer staff to their supplier(s) (Figure 4.8).

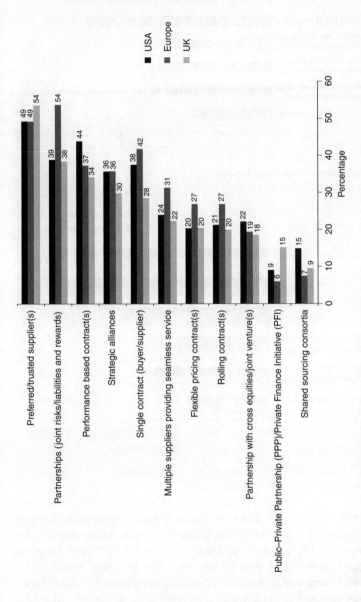

Figure 4.6 Future outsourcing arrangements: international comparison.
Note: Respondents selected multiple options.

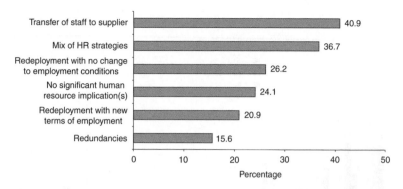

Figure 4.7   Future HR arrangements.
Note: Respondents selected multiple options.

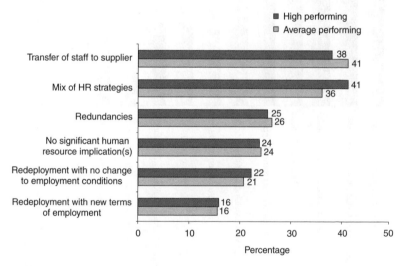

Figure 4.8   Future HR arrangements: best run companies.
Note: Respondents selected multiple options.

International comparison of the arrangements companies will negotiate on behalf of those employees affected by outsourcing does display
differences of likely future practice between US, UK and European
companies. Transfer of staff to suppliers and adopting a mix of HR
strategies, is favoured by US and UK companies (Figure 4.9). In contrast,
European companies predict that outsourcing in the future will lead to
greater redundancies than at present. Further, a considerable number of
UK companies consider that there are likely to be no significant HR

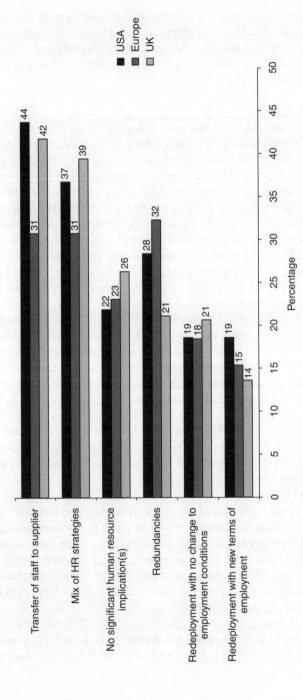

Figure 4.9 Future HR arrangements: international comparison.
Note: Respondents selected multiple options.

implications emerging from outsourcing, as the redeployment that takes place will involve change of employer but not changes in employment conditions for staff and management. In contrast, US companies consider that redeployment with new terms of employment conditions is more likely in the future.

Outsourcing what?

The IT services and HR-based processes and activities are likely to receive the greatest attention in terms of outsourcing in the future (Figure 4.10). The only key difference from the trends discussed in Chapter 2 is that IT outsourcing is predicted to become more prominent in the future. A considerable number of respondents commented that IT-based activities and services will continue to be high on the list of outsourcing priorities due to the rapid advances in technology. Once innovative developments become commercially available, a new wave of IT outsourcing will start. In contrast, HR outsourcing is predicted to be a popular target for a period of time. Once the objectives of HR outsourcing have been achieved, HR systems and processes will no longer be a prime area of concern for outsourcing.

A second cluster of processes, functions and activities that are identified as particular areas for future outsourcing, include basic services (canteen, cleaning services), e-commerce-related processes/activities, facilities management and telecommunication services. The outsourcing of other functions, such as logistics, accounting services, purchasing and back-office processing fall lower on the list of priorities. The emphasis given in the literature to the outsourcing of manufacturing (see Chapter 2) is viewed as unlikely to continue as it falls particularly low on the list of outsourcing priorities. The use of call-centres to facilitate the outsourcing of particular functions and processes is predicted to remain at a similar level as today (see Chapter 2).

Those areas targeted by high- and average-performing companies for outsourcing in the future display a similar trend. High-performing companies predict that greater attention will be given to the outsourcing of IT services and e-commerce related activities followed by HR processes and activities. (Figure 4.11). High-performing companies further indicate that they are more likely to target functions such as finance, purchasing and also back-office processing for outsourcing in the future, than are average-performing companies.

Average-performing companies also report that they will attend to the outsourcing of IT services and HR activities and processes. Average-performing companies will also outsource basic services, facilities

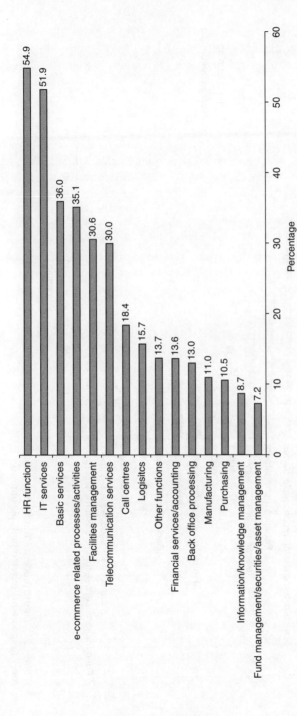

Figure 4.10 Future processes/functions outsourced.
Note: Respondents selected multiple options.

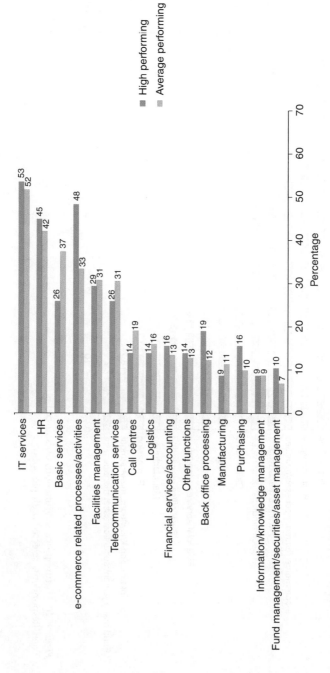

Figure 4.11 Future processes/functions outsourced: best run companies.
Note: Respondents selected multiple options.

management and telecommunication services, namely the more commodity and non-core processes and activities of the organisation, than will high-performing companies. Further, average-performing companies predict that they will make greater use of call-centres than will high-performing companies.

International comparison shows that IT services and HR processes and activities are the two key-target areas for future outsourcing, particularly for US and European companies (Figure 4.12). The UK companies report they are more likely to focus on the outsourcing of IT services and e-commerce-related processes and activities, followed by HR services and activities. The US companies predict they will outsource more basic services, telecommunication services, facilities management, accounting services and purchasing, than the UK and European companies. Although low on the list of priorities, US companies emphasise their greater attention on the outsourcing of information and knowledge management, than UK or European companies. The outsourcing of logistics capabilities is particularly favoured by US and European companies. As with the trends already shown in Figures 4.10 and 4.11, the adoption of call centres will probably remain at the same level as now, with European companies more likely to utilise this facility to enable future outsourcing than US or UK companies.

Keiretsu: the way forward

I think you are going to have fragmented organisations. In fact, you're obviously going to need to revisit what their [the service purchasers'] organisational strategy should or could be in order to understand what functions they really need. I'm sure you will see that there are going to be fewer functions operating inside a form of organisation structure in the future than that you have today – Justin Jewett, CEO, Nestor Healthcare Group Plc

Outsourcing in the future, as identified by the Kakabadse survey and by other writers, researchers and practitioners as Justin Jewitt, emphasises that the present trend of effectively managing a number of horizontal contractual relationships with key trusted suppliers, with each supplier in the chain focusing on providing best-in-class service to give the host organisation competitive advantage, will gain momentum. Enabling the host organisation to gain greater competitive advantage and to be repositioned up the value chain is considered as likely to be

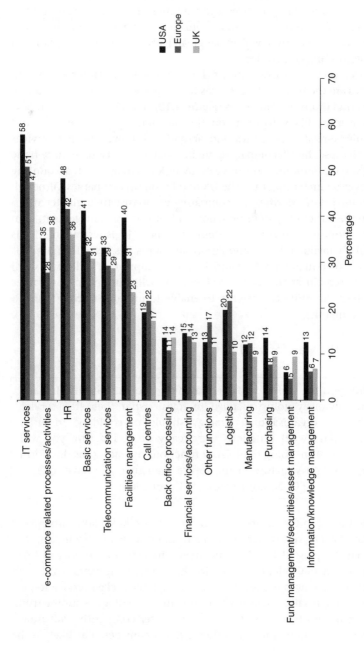

Figure 4.12 Future processes/functions outsourced: international comparison.
Note: Respondents selected multiple options.

achieved by simultaneously pursuing a number of outsourcing strategies, which include improving service quality whilst striving to attain cost advantage and improving efficiency. Such goals will be realised through a variety of outsourcing arrangements, principally with preferred suppliers with whom there exists an established relationship and/or through performance-based contracts. For the best run companies in the future, establishing a meaningful contractual relationship with business partners in order to rapidly improve the quality of goods and services offered to customers, whilst simultaneously attaining a cost advantage, is considered an even greater competitive imperative than now. Such efforts to externalise and become an extended enterprise bear a remarkable resemblance to the Japanese 'keiretsu' model.

Japanese automotive and high technology firms frequently engage in cost sharing with smaller suppliers. Although considered in the West as vertically integrated companies, or 'related conglomerates' that redeploy certain skills from market to market, Japanese automotive and technology firms are structured around 'mother companies'. The 'mother company' is primarily concerned with arranging for design and assembly through a number of independent suppliers and alliance partners, but without owning such satellite enterprises. This long-standing and successful subcontracting culture is based on intercompany cooperation. Such relationships, common in many Japanese manufacturing firms, has accounted for approximately 48 per cent of the configurational structures of all Japanese enterprises. The traditional subcontracting alliance, or 'keiretsu', is built on the principle of long-term partnership, trust, information exchange and through limiting the impact of competitive pressure on suppliers. 'Keiretsu' organisations have been configured as vertically linked industrial conglomerates, as they are integrated through their vertical base to suppliers and distributors and horizontally to banks and trading companies. Keiretsu based enterprises are accustomed to managing long-standing relationships involving explicit (equity holdings) and implicit (reputational) aspects. 'Keiretsu' type relationships are considered to enable greater focus and business discipline for the benefits of the partners by the partners. This is because they create conditions that permit suppliers to make the investments that will help them to accelerate through their learning curve of providing high-quality service, principally through showing them the advantages of having a volume based and lower cost-per-unit-based relationship with the 'mother company'. Such a series of interwoven relationships encourages longer term planning, supports investment and promotes a culture of innovation. Meeting specific needs through innovative practice whilst pursuing economies of scale has been acclaimed as the outcome of keiretsu interlinkages.

Despite the economic downturn in Japan, largely brought about by not following keiretsu principles and by speculative investments in real estate, the keiretsu way of working is considered as an emerging influential force in determining sourcing arrangements in western countries. The Kakabadse survey results show that to improve relationships with suppliers and manage outsourcing contracts effectively, the operational and strategic capabilities required to achieve high-quality outsourcing, outlined in Chapter 3, will remain in vogue for the foreseeable future. However, two additional outsourcing capabilities are identified as important in managing future sourcing arrangements. These are adopting a keiretsu 'mindset' in the management of outsourcing contracts and managing network-based configurations. The Kakabadse survey identifies four elements to adopting a keiretsu mindset:

1   achieving economies of scale through improved supply chain management;
2   delivering economies of scale through new technology;
3   improving transparency of information between business partners;
4   instituting appropriate governance processes and controls in order to attain high quality contractual relationships.

Effectively managing relationships in network-like structures will involve,

- skillfully administering consortia-based arrangements;
- inviting consultancy support;
- being flexible about entering into ever more complex partnership and joint venture arrangements;
- being responsive to any new organisational forms that may emerge.

Table 4.2 displays that the senior managers of high- and average-performing companies consider keiretsu qualities as important for managing

Table 4.2   Importance of Keiretsu: best run companies

	High performing	Average performing
Yes	✓✓✓	✓✓
No		✓

Note: ✓✓✓ – very important; ✓✓ – important; ✓ – not important.

Table 4.3 Adopting a Keiretsu mindset: best run companies

	High performing	Average performing
• Economies of scale through improved supply chain management	✓✓	✓✓
• Economies of scale through new technology	✓✓✓	✓✓✓
• Improving transparency of information between partners	✓✓✓	✓✓✓
• Instituting governance process/controls	✓	✓

Note: ✓✓✓ – very capable; ✓✓ – capable; ✓ – not capable.

a network of horizontal supplier relationships in the future. Concerning the level of capability to apply keiretsu ways of working, Table 4.3 shows the responses from senior managers from both high- and average-performing companies. The senior managers of both groups of companies indicate that they are well prepared to achieve economies of scale through improved supply chain management and through greater utilisation of new technology. Also, the willingness and ability to bring about greater openness of communication between the partners is considered as high. The one area considered problematic by both high- and average-performing companies is instituting appropriate governance procedures and controls acceptable to all the key parties. Two reasons emerge as to why the practice of governance in the future is viewed as challenging, namely, having the parties involved agree on what is to be monitored and applying monitoring procedures in a manner that is acceptable.

A similar pattern of response emerges concerning the capabilities required to manage future network configurations (Table 4.4). Managers from both high- and average-performing companies recognise the relevance of each of the four network configurational skills and report only slight differences of level of preparedness by their organisation to apply such skills. High-performing companies indicate that they will be well prepared to manage consortia-based arrangements. Average-performing companies report a lower level of preparedness for managing consortia-based relationships. In contrast, managers from average-performing companies indicate that they are more likely to utilise the services of outsourcing consultants than are the managers of high-performing companies. Furthermore, the managers of high-performing companies report that they will be better prepared to be responsive to new and

Table 4.4 New network configurations: best run companies

	High performing	Average performing
• Administering consortia-based arrangements	✓✓✓	✓✓
• Use of consultants	✓	✓✓
• Partnerships/joint ventures	✓✓✓	✓✓✓
• Responsive to new organisational forms	✓✓✓	✓✓

Note: ✓✓✓ – very capable; ✓✓ – capable; ✓ – not capable.

enterprising contractual relationships and outsourcing structures than managers of average-performing companies. However, all managers in the survey concur that they will, in the future, be more prepared to adopt partnership and joint venture arrangements according to what is appropriate for each programme of outsourcing.

International comparison reveals virtually no difference of response between US, UK and European companies concerning the adoption of a keiretsu mindset to future outsourcing and being prepared to manage the new network relationships and structures (Tables 4.5 and 4.6). The US, UK and European companies report that they will have the capability to achieve greater economies of scale in the future through improved supply chain management.

However, UK companies report that they will be less prepared to achieve economies of scale through the sourcing of new technology than the US and European companies. Further, and similar to the responses from high- and average-performing companies, UK, US and European firms highlight the difficulty they expect to experience in instituting appropriate governance procedures and controls to outsourcing arrange-

Table 4.5 Adopting a Keiretsu mindset: international comparison

	UK	Europe	USA
• Economies of scale through improved supply chain management	✓✓✓	✓✓✓	✓✓✓
• Economies of scale through new technology	✓✓	✓✓✓	✓✓✓
• Improving transparency of information between partners	✓✓✓	✓✓✓	✓✓✓
• Instituting governance process and controls	✓	✓	✓

Note: ✓✓✓ – very capable; ✓✓ – capable; ✓ – not capable.

Table 4.6 New network configurations: international comparison

	UK	Europe	USA
• Administering consortia-based arrangements	✓✓	✓✓	✓✓
• Use of consultants	✓	✓	✓
• Partnerships/joint ventures	✓✓✓	✓✓✓	✓✓✓
• Responsive to new organisational forms	✓✓✓	✓✓✓	✓✓✓

Note: ✓✓✓ – very capable; ✓✓ – capable; ✓ – not capable.

ments and relationships. The same reasons are quoted, namely, agreeing on a set of procedures which are acceptable to all partners and then agreeing how such arrangements are to be policed. Also, US, UK and European companies report that they are unlikely to use the services of outsourcing consultants. Additionally, US, UK and European companies indicate that they need to improve their capability to manage consortia-based relationships. A strong convergence of opinion emerges, emphasising that, to facilitate relationships with trusted suppliers through performance based, partnership type arrangements, keiretsu and network-based capabilities will be necessary.

Summary

Research to date

- A mix of reasons for outsourcing in the future are identified, including the need to reduce costs, focus on the core competences of the organisation, enhance the quality of service to customers, gain greater competitive advantage and help improve the organisation's position in the value chain.
- Different forms of sourcing relationships are likely to emerge which involve a greater sharing of risk between partners.

The Kakabadse survey results

- The reasons for undertaking outsourcing in the future are considered to remain similar to current practice (see Chapter 2), such as, aiming to achieve best practice, promoting a greater sense of cost discipline in the organisation, improving levels of service quality and focusing more on the core competencies of the organisation, all in order to gain greater competitive advantage.
- Greater use is likely to be made of new technology through outsourcing.

- Similar trends emerge to the predicted future generic trends when comparing high-performing with average-performing companies. However, there are some differences between high- and average-performing companies outlined below.
- High-performing companies report their intention to source new technology in order to achieve greater economies of scale and to help management to focus more on the core competences of the organisation.
- High-performing companies indicate that in order to enhance their position in the value chain, management's capability to drive through change requires improvement.
- Similar trends emerge when undertaking an international comparison, except that European companies report a greater preference for sourcing new technology and for instituting cost discipline procedures and practices in the organisation.
- Similar to the present day practices discussed in Chapter 2, future outsourcing relationships are likely to be pursued with preferred suppliers with whom a trusting relationship has been established.
- Greater preference in the future is predicted to be given to performance-based contracts with suppliers.
- It is reported that more partnership-based arrangements are likely in the future.
- High-performing companies predict that their future outsourcing arrangements are more likely to involve performance-based contracts with multiple suppliers as part of a network of strategic alliances.
- The US companies indicate that they will adopt performance-based contracts but with preferred suppliers, whilst European companies indicate they will give greater preference to partnerships which share risks, liabilities and rewards and to single contract arrangements.
- The UK companies highlight that they are likely to pursue relationships with existing, preferred suppliers.
- Similar to the trends identified in Chapter 2, future arrangements for employees affected by outsourcing are likely to involve transferring staff to suppliers and adopting a mix of HR strategies to suit the circumstances of each outsourcing contract.
- High-performing companies indicate a greater preference for adopting a mix of HR strategies, whilst average-performing companies prefer outsourcing arrangements which directly transfer staff to suppliers.
- International comparison highlights that US and UK companies will transfer more staff to suppliers and also adopt a mix of strategies to

suit the circumstances, whilst European companies will probably pursue a policy of redundancies, as a result of outsourcing.

- HR-based activities and processes and IT services are identified as the two key areas for outsourcing in the future.
- High-performing companies predict they will attend more to outsourcing IT services, e-commerce related activities and the HR processes and activities.
- International comparison predicts that US companies will attend more to outsourcing IT services, HR processes and activities, basic services and those activities involved in facilities management.
- European companies indicate that they will utilise more call-centres to support outsourcing, than US and UK companies.
- To ensure successful outsourcing in the future, companies will need the capability to form keiretsu type relationships between the host organisation and suppliers.

References and further reading

For further information on the concept of paradigm, read Kuhn (1970). For an explanation of paradigm boundaries and definition of meanings, read Barker (1992).

For an examination of the paradigm shift taking place in outsourcing and its impact on organisational structures, read Spitzer (1999), Barker (1992), Heller (1996) and Hein (1997).

For further insights into Keiretsu structures and networked relationships, read Helper and Sako (1995) and Dyer and Ouchi (1993).

For an economic analysis of the conditions which lead to the formation of oligopolistic corporations, see Sweezy (1997), Leatt et al. (1997), Seurat (1999) and Rothery and Robertson (1995).

For greater understanding of the transition from vertically integrated enterprises to more horizontal, contractually driven networks, see Kutnick (1999), Leisman (1999) and Rowley (1999).

For more information on Japanese automotive and high technology firms, see Asanuma and Kikutani (1992) and Kawaski and McMillan (1987).

For achieving greater economy of scale practices and for investment in and the development of supply chain management skills, see Dyer and Ouchi (1993) and Chalos and Sung (1998). For insights into 'alliance capitalism', namely Keiretsu structures, in terms of cross shareholdings, see Aoki and Dore (1996) and Thomas and Waring (1999). For more information on the mother company concept, see Rumelt (1974), Davidson (1983) and Chalos and Sung (1998).

For a view as to the transferability of the Keiretsu concept to the Western context, see Lewis (1995), Domberger (1998), Kakabadse and Kakabadse (1999; 2000a), Ring and Van de Van (1992), Quinn (1999) and Lorenzoni and Baden-Fuller (1995).

For further information on the impact of outsourcing on employees and the consequent HR arrangements likely to be adopted, read Labib and Appelbaum (1993), Laabs (1998), Losey (1998) and West and Patterson (1998).

5
The Public Services

Case study: Alun Cole, senior partner, Morgan Cole Co (Solicitors)

Views on Outsourcing in Public Services

In the private sector,...the driver is either profit or strategic goals....In the public sector, it can be political, which may not make commercial sense, but may well make political sense....Some of the earlier privatisations were commercially unsound....I don't think that outsourcing in the private sector will ever be driven by any equivalent ideology. The development of suitable methodologies for the outsourcing of public services has been very slow, in part because it has been heavily influenced by the dictates and the vagaries of politics. Early privatisations and PFIs (private finance initiatives), in particular, were very ideologically driven. The early methodologies were also extremely mechanistic and formula bound, and that often meant that unless the service schemes to which they were to be applied had been well selected (which, on the whole, they were not), all kinds of distortions and manipulations had to be undertaken in order to make them fit the prescribed outsourcing criteria. Poor selection, and the long lead times necessary to secure financial and legal close of the transactions (often exacerbated by the 'distortions and manipulations') meant that many of the service schemes selected for outsourcing, could not be sustained.

Alun Cole, senior partner of Morgan Cole Solicitors and formerly a UK government legal adviser at both the Home Office and the Welsh Office,

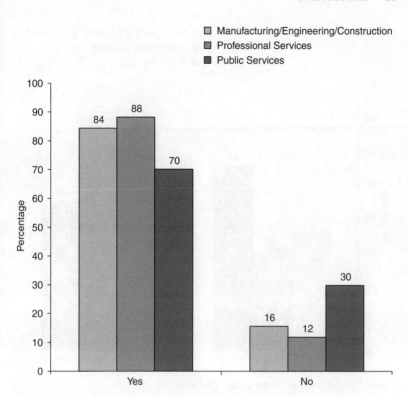

Figure 5.1 Managers influence on the purchase of outsourcing services.

who takes a lead role on behalf of his legal practice in advising both the public and the private sector on the law and practice of outsourcing, draws a sharp distinction between private sector and public service organisation approaches towards outsourcing. He refers to a particular dimension to outsourcing in the public services, namely political influence. He continues, '... sometimes government bodies have been driven to outsource where it actually does not make good sense, so it will inevitably produce a bad result'.

The point being made is that a substantial proportion of outsourcing decisions have been taken out of the hands of the managers of public service organisations and have been determined by the political process for reasons other than what is of direct value to the organisation.

The Alun Cole perspective is supported by the Kakabadse Survey results. Comparing the influence public service managers have on outsourcing decisions against that of managers from professional services

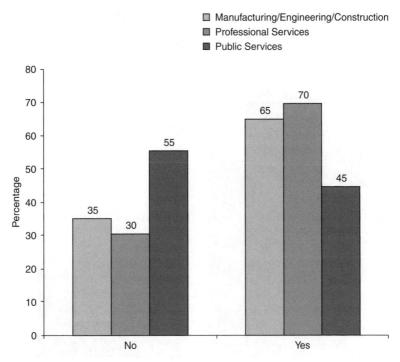

Figure 5.2 Value from outsourcing: shared view at the top.

firms (i.e. consulting services, software services) and managers from the manufacturing, engineering and construction sectors confirms that public service managers are less able to determine the purchase of outsourcing services than managers of companies from the other sectors (Figure 5.1). In fact, 30 per cent of top managers of public service organisations report that they have no direct influence on the purchase of outsource services. Further, 55 per cent of public service managers report that no value has been gained from outsourcing (Figure 5.2). The managers of public service organisations emerge as the most sceptical about the benefits of outsourcing.

The view that little value is gained from outsourcing in the public services is expressed by managers who display a longer tenure of employment than that of managers of organisations in the other sectors. Fifty-four per cent of public service managers report that they have been with their organisation for over ten years (Figure 5.3). Length of tenure in any one role is similar across the sectors. Managers from public service organisations, professional services, manufacturing, engineering and construction

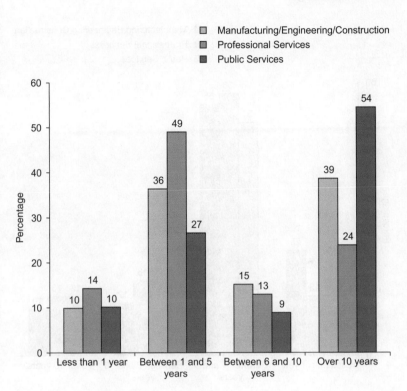

Figure 5.3 Organisation tenure.

companies are likely to change jobs within a period of between one and five years (Figure 5.4). The survey suggests that the senior managers of public service organisations are likely to have as much, if not more insight about the needs of their organisation, than do their counterparts in companies from other sectors. Managers of public service organisations may have held more different jobs in their organisation than the managers from the other sectors, but they have remained with the one organisation for a considerable period of time. Hence, the negativity concerning the value of outsourcing is likely to arise from as intimate and as accurately held a view concerning the current and future requirements of the organisation, as managers from companies from other sectors.

To throw light on how such differences of view can arise from well-experienced managers, this chapter explores developments in public services administration and management following the Second World War. It is argued that post-war liberalism has been replaced by a philosophy

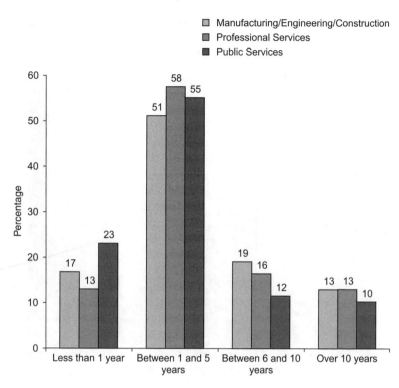

Figure 5.4   Role tenure.

of 'value-for-money', which has led to a revolution in the management of the public services, initially in the developed countries and now increasingly in the developing countries. The re-engineering of the public services through privatisation and outsourcing have produced 'leaner' organisations that are considered more cost effective but face the criticism of now providing diminishing levels of quality of service. In fact, the argument that certain underprivileged groups derive little benefit from government and the public services is gaining momentum. To clarify the impact of the restructuring agenda on the public services, the Kakabadse survey examines how outsourcing is influencing the structure and running of public service organisations and the quality of services provided. As already stated, comparison is made with organisations from professional services, manufacturing, engineering and construction in order to benchmark the impact of outsourcing in the public services. In particular, attention is given to examining the services being outsourced, the reasons for outsourcing, the preferred service providers utilised and the nature of the contractual relationship between them and the host organisation. Further, the capabilities of public service managers to manage outsourcing contracts are compared with those of managers from professional services and manufacturing, engineering and construction companies. The chapter concludes by exploring the impact of outsourcing on the performance of public service organisations and the quality of their relationship with their suppliers.

Developments in the public services

The negative view of outsourcing in public services organisations has its roots in the changes that have taken place in the philosophy and practice of management in the public services over the last four decades.

Post-Second World War, the focus of public policy has been to structure national and local government institutions to offer a variety of public services which are accessible to all citizens. Much of the literature of the day assumed a 'policy orientation', namely a concern with how political and public servants can make available high-quality public services to their populace. In delivering such services, public organisations assumed traditional, hierarchical structures. Irrespective of whether public services were wholly or partly subsidised by government, large, hierarchical public bodies were the norm for most developed economies such as the United States of America, United Kingdom, Canada, Australia and New Zealand. However, the United Kindom broke out of this mould earlier than other governments.

Liberal governments of the last two decades have been pressing for fundamental structural change. Since the mid 1980s, the vertically integrated philosophy and service praxis of public administration has been increasingly replaced by the notion of a public sector that should provide 'value for money'. In response to a world economy characterised by transnational markets and the need for enterprises to evolve global structures in order to compete, government has been obliged to act more as a market driven enterprise. The emerging public policy has attempted to integrate public service provision with financial disciplines and display how value for money has been achieved from investment in the public services. Thus, with increasing global competition and changing patterns of employment, and an ever greater demand for personal and community services, the need to find innovative solutions at the local level to complex social problems, such as in the areas of health, housing, community safety and unemployment, has generated pressure to reform and change the public services along the lines of greater control over costs.

These developments have had, and are continuing to have, profound effects on the management of the public services. Indeed, whilst not uniformly applied, they are part of an emerging movement which has led to a redefinition and transformation, and in some cases a blurring of, the traditional roles of public and private sector organistions. The role of the state in defining, protecting and promoting societal interests has been, and is being, reshaped by a global campaign for value, emerging as privatisation and public services commercialisation. At the root of this global restructuring is a 'techno-economic' influence promoting a range of new organisational possibilities facilitated by information related technology. A world vastly different from that of the mid 1970s, has been created in a relatively short period of time.

Economic globalisation, combined with concepts of value-for-money services, has led politicians to restructure the state and to hive-off certain peripheral functions to agencies in the private sector. Hence, the changes sweeping across the public services of developed and developing economies have reflected a privatisation agenda. The language used has been that of 'flexibility', 'responsiveness', 'deregulation', 're-engineering' and 'quality of service'. Putting these concepts into practice requires visible improvement in productivity, changing skill-base boundaries, greater application of technology and greater interagency networking and community-agency networking. These developments represent more than a manifestation of policies of particular governments. The new value-for-money ideology has given birth to a search for new organisational forms and structures for public service bodies.

In response, politicians, party advisors, and senior civil servants started looking for new solutions to the complex problems of cost management, organisational reconfiguration and service provision. As the key motivation for change in the public services has been to introduce a discipline over the management of costs whilst concurrently improving public sector performance, private sector management techniques became ever more attractive. The philosophy of economic rationalism took a firm grip on public services management.

However, the ever growing prominence of private sector managerial practice in public service organisations provoked considerable disquiet and opposition. A still politically influential opinion argues that public administration is under threat from the alien paradigm of commercial management. The initiative for change, which the anti-commercialisation lobby believes to be politically motivated in order to reengineer public service organisations and nurture new structures and mechanisms for service delivery, has led to the deregulation of the labour market and the 'privatisation' of public sector authorities. There has been a strong move to replace centralised industrial relations mechanisms with labour contracts based on enterprise performance and small group or individual bargaining. The proponents of the new public service order argue that public service employees should be as independent from the encumbrance of formal organisations as possible and that this independence should be achieved through sub-contracting, franchising and payment based on piece work and/or incentive payments. This is a fundamental shift from the career-based public service which, until recently, was arguably the single dominant source of continuation of employment in government.

In contrast to the deregulation of the labour market, governments have maintained control over the processes and activities that have been sold off or outsourced. The British government 'denationalised' huge chunks of public services and voluntary activities, but continued to maintain control over the finances and structure of the new agency entities through quangos. However, attempting to maintain financial controls whilst deregulating agency structures, generating quasi markets, promoting performance related pay for the staff and managers of the agencies and pursuing improvements in quality of service through the expansion of the audit inspection, has also created tension between the disciplines that drive centrally based controls and the discretions that are exercised through decentralisation. The result is that many civil servants and their departments are left with the daunting task of implementing a never ending stream of reforms which in private are often viewed as fads. Similarly, a growing body of commentators and researchers have questioned the value of applying the 'business management approach' to public administration. The strongly held view is that 'managerialism' does not promote a clear set of principles, other than cost reduction, on which to organise public services.

> So the pressing issue for local authorities and, I think, the public sector more generally, is we have got a legacy of under investment that we have to deal with. Yet, at the same time, we have greater public expectation that public services will improve in the front line, schools will be better. More money will be available to social services, roads will be repaired. So we've got to face up to different ways of finding investment to bring to the Council – David Bell, CEO, Bedfordshire County Council, UK

Despite misgivings, successive western governments, notably those of the United Kingdom and the United States, have pursued the management agenda with zeal, as reflected in the views expressed by David Bell. Other more conservative governments, such as those of New Zealand, Japan, Sweden and Spain, have equally pursued the agenda of re-positioning their public services. France, which initially resisted the application of private sector management principles, is considered by some to lie ahead of Britain through its rationalisation of the budgetary process. Even China has not been immune to the impact of managerialism. Economic reform, which began in China in the late 1980s, was aimed at overcoming bureaucratic inertia. The reforms led to a devolution of resource allocation from central to local governments, allowing heads of regional government to distribute considerable proportions of state revenue. The decentralisation of authority has encouraged managers to accept managerial accountability, which in turn has eroded the influence and authority of 'the politicracts'. Also, the influence of economic management has extended to Eastern European economies, where foreign experts have been called in to advise on the outsourcing of particular activities and processes, leading to the establishment in certain countries of special purpose ministries separate from the traditional bureaucracy.

The reason for the disquiet over privatisation, restructuring and outsourcing amongst public service managers is primarily one of philosophy, captured in the private gain vs. public good arguments. Table 5.1

Table 5.1 Private sector gain vs. public service provision

Organisation	Private sector	Public service
Purpose	• Profit-driven • Market values • Economic objectives	• Geo-political driven • Social values • Contrasting objectives
Economic context	• Competitive markets	• Market/Community interaction
	• Accountable to shareholders	• Publicly accountable
	• Liquidity and capital	• Taxation
Management strategies	• Flexible/Discretionary	• Prescriptive • Regulation
	• Risk orientation	• Legislation • Predefined goals
	• Goal setting	

Source: Compiled from Korac-Kakabadse and Korac-Kakabadse (1997).

shows the differences between private and public services philosophy and practice.

These differences of purpose and goal orientation between private sector and public service organisations makes the management of change as between these two types of bodies a strikingly different experience. Public service bodies are socio/politically driven, whereas private sector organisations have clearer revenue and profit driven motivation. Public service bodies have to account for multiple objectives simultaneously whilst also being conscious of the reaction of numerous stakeholders. Most private sector organiations have the flexibility to work to a set of clearer goals to satisfy shareholder aspirations. Managing change within public service organisations, particularly those concerned with the provision of social services, requires nurturing and influencing key stakeholders in order to reduce the potential conflicts of interest that exist within a complex web of political and interagency relationships. Proposals for change need to be laid out for consultation and account taken of the responses, so that the support of most stakeholders has been agreed prior to officials 'going to market'. Thus change management and the everyday experience of managing multiple stakeholders have become synonymous. Managing reform in public service organisations requires attention to the organisation/multiple stakeholder interface, as well as to the quality of relationships between stakeholders, irrespective of whether the stakeholders have a legitimate source of interest in the enterprise. To neglect certain stakeholders could have damaging political and service delivery repercussions.

Thus, management in the public services can be viewed as the management of a community of stakeholders with interlocking political and resource interests. It is understandable that in circumstances of clarifying ways forward through the conflicting priorities of various stakeholder groups, particularly when demand for services is increasing and resources decreasing, the attraction of outsourcing in order for management to concentrate on core activities, has been overwhelming.

Outsourcing: IT led reform

For public service organisations privatisation and outsourcing have gone hand in hand. Government pressure and legislative requirements have both encouraged and forced public services organisations to put their services out to competitive tender. Such has been the case with the UK's Local Government Act, 1998, which made competitive tendering for local authority services compulsory. Similarly, the OECD's Best Practice Guide for Contracting Government Services states that in-house bids should in all respects be treated the same as external bids and that all bids should detail all of the items necessary to realise the desired service. In such a climate, the predominant view has been that gains in productivity, particularly through the use of technology, driven as much by the need to reduce costs, is the right way forward.

Hence, over the last decade, particular attention has been given to IT outsourcing amongst public service organisations. In Australia, for example, many public service senior executives have 're-engineered' their departments in order to cut costs. The Australian Federal Government had embarked, from the mid-1980s, on a road of public service and industrial reform that was technology led. Australian government initiatives brought about work restructuring, initially to the public services, and later to industry through the adoption of information systems technology. The 1993 Australian government review of the public sector emphasised the importance of IT led reform by concluding that IT was a fundamental enabler for increasing government competitiveness. The 1995 Government Information Technology Review Group, which scrutinised 97 per cent of public sector organisations, identified considerable opportunities for taking advantage of IT developments.

Similarly, the Canadian Government's 1994 enquiry report concluded that IT is fundamental to the development of public sector competitiveness. Likewise the US Government's 1993 National Performance Review suggested a need for re-engineering the whole business of government through the use of IT. The report further suggested that the American Federal Government, with the exception of the Defence Department, was significantly behind the private sector in identifying and applying the latest information systems technology and was virtually the only sector of American society yet to confront the need to reinvent itself for the information age. At state level, the 1994 report of the State of California's Task Force on Government Technology Policy and Procurement, recommended an increase in the state's IT budget in the face of reductions in the state's budget. The Task Force also identified a lack of enterprise-wide planning and coordination in IT, a lack of performance information and a lengthy delivery time for solutions.

In a similar vein, the Swedish Government's 1994 Commission on IT promoted the use of IT as a prime means of improving the quality of life and of its citizens and the nation's competitiveness internationally. The report made a series of recommendations on what had to be achieved and through which means in areas such as education, research, the legal system, and public administration. The Danish Government outlined a strategy for the year 2000 which covered issues such as health, data protection and privacy, education, libraries, mass media, telecommunications and the impact of IT on the working life of the Danish people. Thus the role of IT in public service has evolved from that of an administrative support tool to that of a catalyst for radical change.

The arrangements concerning outsourcing through IT are that IT contracts are more geared towards managed service deals, through partnership arrangements. Market research conducted by ITNet in 1999 established that partnerships require sensitivity to the style and culture of each partner. On this note, the view that is considered to have emerged amongst public service managers is that partners listening to each other and working closer to develop joint project skills requires greater investment in training and development in order to better manage supplier relationships. The demand for better training is understandable, as for example, the market size for IT outsourcing in local government in the United Kingdom in 1998 was reported to be worth £124 million, an increase of 15.6 per cent on the previous year.

However, processes, functions and activities other than IT are increasingly being considered for outsourcing. In 1997, the OECD reported that a wide range of activities were being outsourced in the public sector, ranging from international airport operations by the city of Indianapolis in the United States of America, to IT based activities by the UK's Inland Revenue and its counterpart in Australia, the Australian Tax Office, to internal audit functions by the New Zealand Audit Office, to cleaning services by the Copenhagen National Hospital, Denmark.

In contrast to the comments by Alun Cole and to the findings of the Kakabadse survey, it has also been reported that outsourcing is having a positive impact. A 1995 review of outsourcing arrangements in Australia, New Zealand and the United Kingdom, carried out by the Australian Department of Finance, reported an improvement in both public service organisation/client relationships and government decision making. Further, a 1996 study by the Australian Industry Commission identified improvements in quality of service delivery resulting from greater specialisation through the outsourcing of particular non-core activities and by also being able to effectively monitor service providers. In addition, a 1996 study of English local authorities indicated that as a result of outsourcing, 7 per cent to 10 per cent cost savings were being achieved.

Irrespective of whether outsourcing has had a positive impact or not, as Table 5.2 suggests, the growth in outsourcing in government is substantial, reaching the point where public service and private sector organisations are increasingly competing to provide government funded services. Joint ventures are being formed for the ownership and operation of infrastructure programmes. Further, certain arrangements have gone beyond private financing type initiatives (PFIs). Service providers are paid according to performance/partnership based formulae. Such has been the case in the United Kingdom, between the Employment Services and EDS, whereby EDS is remunerated for achieving particular business benefits through an arrangement known as business benefit based contracting.

Another development amongst government agencies has been the 'best value' or 'value for money' approach to outsourcing. The best value concept had its roots in the US Department of Defence's Planning,

Table 5.2   Recent outsourcing contracts with government

Customer	Contract value	Supplier	Year signed
Inland Revenue UK	$1.5 bn	EDS	1994
Australian Commonwealth Bank (50% Government owned)	AUS$500 m and purchased of 35% equity stake in vendor	EDS	1997
Telstra, Australia	AUS$130 m	IBM	1998
Department of Trade and Industry, UK	$330 m	ICL	1998
Passport Agency	$220 m	Siemens	1998
Department of Social Services, UK Local Government	$500 m	Sema Group	1998
Australian Taxation Office	AUS$20 m	EDS	1999
Department of Social Security (DSS)	$3.3 bn plus incentive of $2.5 bn*	Electronic Data Services (EDS) consortium	2000
US Navy Marine Corps	$4.9 bn plus incentive of $2.8 bn**	Electronic Data Services (EDS)	2000

Source: Compiled from *Dataquest* (1999), Foremski (2000), *Agence France Presse* (2000).
* World's second largest IT outsourcing contract; ** Largest US Government IT outsourcing contract.

Programming and budgeting System (PPBS) initiative that the then Defence Secretary, Robert S. McNamara, brought to the Pentagon from General Motors. The PPBS initiative has continued without fundamental change for over 38 years and through eight government administrations, both Democrat and Republican. In keeping with the best value philosophy, UK local authorities are expected to benchmark their own performance against others' including organisations in the private and voluntary sectors, thereby embracing the concept of fair competition as a means of securing efficient and effective services. According to the British Audit Commission Report published in the year 2000 the best value concept is a challenging performance framework that requires local authorities to publish annual best value performance plans and to review the levels of best value attained for all their services, every five years. Authorities must show that they have applied the '4C's' of best value – challenge, compare, compete, consult – to every review and demonstrate to their own communities that they are achieving continuous improvement in all of their services. Similarly, under the Government Performance and Results Act of 1993, federal agencies in the United States of America are required to carry out performance measurement, planning and annual reporting activities. In the United Kingdom, by December 1999, outsourcing type agreements for over 250 PFI projects had been signed by central and local government agencies on best value lines, for the procurement of services across a wide range of sectors which included roads, rail, hospitals, prisons, office accommodations and IT systems, ranging in capital value from less than a million pounds to several billion pounds, amounting to an aggregate capital value of approximately £16 billion.

Although best value measures and benchmarking practices are becoming commonplace with many governments, such as those in the United Kingdom, Australia, Canada and the United States of America, the United Kingdom remains the leading country when it comes to introducing best value-related practices to government agencies. Such emphasis is illustrated by the growing numbers of reports on best value, such as the UK's Treasury's guidance on 'Appraisal and Evaluation in Central Government', published in 1997, the various publications on 'Private Finance Initiatives' (PFI's), and 'Private–Public Partnerships' (PPP), the report on Government Information and Communication Services which emerged in the year 2000, and the emergence of web-pages on value for money. Both Conservative and Labour governments have adopted 'best value' as the guiding principle for government. The Conservative government promoted best value thinking through the

Citizen's Charters, which by 1997 accounted for 42 national and more than 10 000 local charters. Each of these charters was based on principles that dealt with value for money and/or efficient and effective economic delivery of public services within the resources the nation could afford, all set against an independent validation of performance according to agreed standards. In fact, the UK's Labour Government programme has more concentrated on best value, by requiring programmes of activity to be measured against key drivers, namely, risk transfer, the long term nature of contracts (including whole life costing), the use of output-based specifications, competitive tendering, performance measurements and incentives and private sector management skills.

One consequence of the growth in government based outsourcing is the loss of business opportunities for small to medium sized IT firms. For example, in Australia, IBM, EDS and CSC (Cisco Systems Corporation) are reported as the top suppliers of outsourcing services, with IBM holding over AUD$5 billion worth of investments, driven by IBM Global Services, Australian and Advantra, an IBM joint venture, partnered by Telstra and Land Lease Corp. The smaller firms, who in the past had the opportunity to bid for government contracts, are now finding themselves squeezed out by the multinationals. The fear is that such developments are now placing the large providers in the position of acting as governments themselves.

The Kakabadse survey

Services outsourced

Despite the attention given to IT outsourcing in the literature, the most popular area for outsourcing by public service organisations is that of basic services, comparable to the levels reported by manufacturing, engineering and construction companies (Figure 5.5). However, greater emphasis is given to the outsourcing of IT and telecommunication services by public service organisations, than by professional services, manufacturing, engineering and construction companies. An additional area for outsourcing in the public services is facilities management. In effect, outsourcing within public service organisations emerges as concentrating on basic organisational processes such as the management of canteens and that of information systems. Although low on the list of priorities, the outsourcing of e-commerce related processes and activities and accounting services is favoured most by professional services organisations and least by public service bodies.

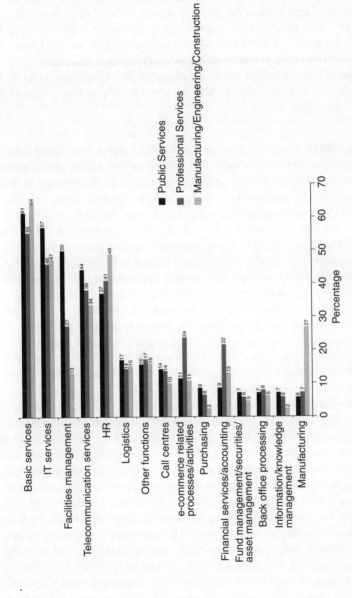

Figure 5.5 Functions, activities, processes outsourced: sector comparison.
Note: Respondents selected multiple options.

Reasons for outsourcing

> Both BBA and Channel 4 have engaged in a substantial amount of outsourcing and I think the primary drivers in both cases can really be put down to a lack of resource in a particular field...at that particular time...I don't believe that outsourcing in the disciplines that we are talking about is driven as much by cost reduction as by seeking to achieve best practice... – Vanni Treeves, Chairman, London Business School, Chairman, BBA Group Plc, Chairman, Channel Four Television.

As indicated by Vanni Treeves, and similar to organisations from other sectors, the survey results show that public service organisations have pursued outsourcing for a number of purposes. Four key reasons for outsourcing are identified, namely, aim to achieve best practice, improve the cost discipline skills of public service managers and tighten up the control processes in the organisation, improve on levels of service quality and to help senior managers more clearly focus on the core competencies of the organisation (Figure 5.6). In comparison to organisations from professional services, manufacturing engineering and construction, public service bodies report that they are more likely to concurrently pursue these four strategies. Professional services, for example, place far greater emphasis on aiming to achieve best practice, whilst companies from manufacturing, engineering and construction concentrate more on achieving cost advantage through outsourcing. Only professional services organisations report that outsourcing enhances their ability to develop new products and services.

Despite attempting to introduce greater cost discipline into the organisation, whilst equally aiming to achieve best practice, improving service quality and attempting to provide best value through greater focus on core competences, outsourced processes and activities are considered by public service managers as non-critical to the current and future functioning of the organisation (Figure 5.7). Irrespective of the diminished levels of importance attributed to outsourcing, its impact is recognised as affecting most or all of the organisation. Further, public service managers, more than managers from companies in the other sectors, consider most of what is outsourced as holding commodity status and supported by mature technology. In contrast, senior managers from professional services, manufacturing, engineering and construction companies view the outsourcing of processes

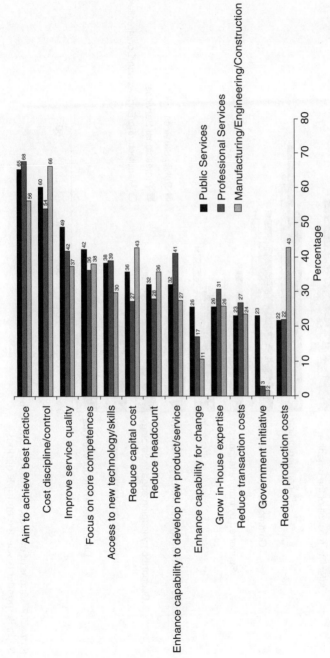

Figure 5.6 Sourcing strategies: sector comparison.
Note: Respondents selected multiple options.

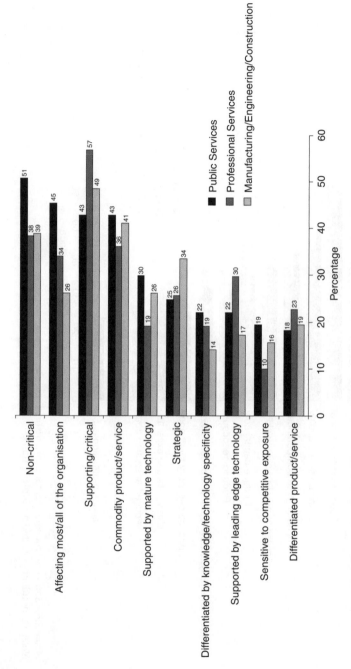

Figure 5.7 Status of outsourced activity: sector comparison.
Note: Respondents selected multiple options.

and activities as critical to their organisation, supporting the key organisational strategies already in place. The outsourcing contracts adopted by professional service organisations are reported as supported by leading edge technology. Professional service organisations also highlight that they gain greater benefit from outsourcing by being enabled to offer competitively differentiated products and services in the market place.

Service providers

> Outsourcing generally involves a great deal of senior management time and can be a strategically risky thing to undertake. Hence it's not the sort of thing one wishes to revisit too often. So it is a development which is undertaken infrequently, but carefully. ... I think long-term relationship building is regarded increasingly as a key element of outsourcing, but with long term relationships there can be vulnerability. The outsourcing body (host organisation) may become more dependent on them ... – Alun Cole, Senior Partner, Morgan Cole, Solicitors

As the volume of outsourcing in public service organisations is increasing, particular attention has been given in the survey to identify which service providers are used most. The findings support the trends identified in Chapter 2, namely, that preferred service providers are those organisations which have a proven track record in particular areas of outsourcing and who also have experience of working with public service organisations (Figure 5.8). As Alun Cole suggests, it takes time to build an effective working relationship. However, the major IT service providers, such as IBM, EDS, SAIC, are ranked higher on the list of preferred service providers than is reported in Chapter 2, supporting the trends outlined by other businesses and academic writers, namely that the more substantial contracts are being serviced by a limited number of large organisation service providers. Alun Cole equally hints at the danger, reported by other writers, that service providers can 'almost become governments themselves'. In contrast, professional service organisations indicate they prefer the smaller niche and ISPs.

Capability comparison

Similar to the analysis of managerial capability for outsourcing between high performing and average performing companies discussed in

142

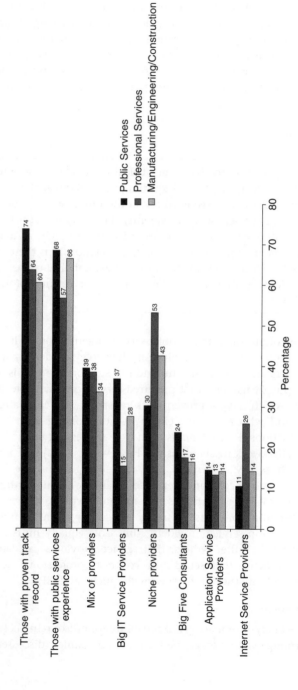

Figure 5.8 Preferred service providers: sector comparison.
Note: Respondents selected multiple options.

Chapter 3, comparison is made between public services organisations and companies in professional services, manufacturing, engineering and construction. The capabilities examined include the degree to which the managers of public services organisations and managers of professional services organisations, engineering, manufacturing and construction companies are skilled at:

• integrating different ways of working within their own organisation and between their organisation and external suppliers;
• preparing the organisation to become outsource ready;
• managing the transactional elements of outsourcing;
• managing supplier relationships;
• managing staff and lower level management in the host organisation.

As far as the skills to integrate different ways of working are concerned, similar patterns of response emerge (Table 5.3) Rearranging ways of working in order to accommodate outsourcing initiatives and being able to integrate different ways of working around activities already outsourced, emerges as being at comparable levels of management capability across the sectors. Applying quality controls through benchmarking against known quality standards emerges as an equally held capability across these different types of organisations.

The capability of senior managers to prepare their organisation to become outsource ready is comparable across the sectors (Table 5.4). The skills to clearly target which processes and activities should be

Table 5.3 Integrating ways of working: sector comparison

Capability	Sector		
Integrative skills	Public service	Professional services	Manufacturing, engineering, construction
Rearrange ways of working	✓✓	✓✓	✓✓
Integrate around activities already outsourced	✓✓	✓✓	✓✓
Benchmark against quality standards	✓✓	✓✓	✓✓
Apply quality controls	✓✓	✓✓	✓✓

Note: ✓✓✓ – well prepared; ✓✓ – prepared; ✓ – poorly prepared.

Table 5.4   Becoming outsource ready: sector comparison

Capability	Sector		
Outsource ready	Public services	Professional services	Manufacturing, engineering, construction
Clear targeting	✓✓	✓✓	✓✓
Level of outsource experience	✓✓	✓✓	✓✓
Risk management capability	✓✓✓	✓✓	✓✓
Managing the transition	✓✓	✓✓✓	✓✓
Outsource strategy integrated with organisation strategy	✓✓	✓✓✓	✓✓
Staff briefings	✓	✓	✓
Resourcing all phases of outsourcing initiatives	✓	✓	✓
Contingency management	✓✓	✓✓	✓

Note: ✓✓✓ – well prepared; ✓✓ – prepared; ✓ – poorly prepared.

outsourced, and the risk management capability to assess the impact of outsourcing, are reported as well developed. Further, the managers of the companies across the sectors report that they are able to effectively integrate outsourcing strategies with the organisational strategies pursued by the enterprise. The capability to manage the transition resulting from the transfer of activities and personnel to service providers, is also identified as comparable across the organisations involved in this analysis. The managers across the sectors also indicate that they share similar difficulties in preparing themselves for outsourcing. Recognising the resourcing requirements for the different phases of various outsourcing initiatives, is identified as particularly challenging for all of the managers in the survey. Conducting staff briefings concerning performance standards and other requirements is also experienced as difficult. However, the capability to manage expected or unexpected contingencies is reported as particularly problematic with companies from the manufacturing, engineering and construction sectors.

> I think another skill is the performance management and monitoring skill ... It's about understanding what are those sophisticated mechanisms by which you measure performance. Again, how do you

relate those particular concerns to communities, because they are not always interested in grand things like the Audit Commission performance indicators. They want to know, 'I've got a hole in my road, how quickly is it fixed?' so you've got to have an understanding of the different methods of performance management... – David Bell, CEO, Bedfordshire County Council

Similar experiences are reported by the managers from all sectors concerning the management of the transactional elements of outsourcing (Table 5.5). A particular area that is seen as requiring attention is management's ability to benchmark service level agreements. In terms of monitoring performance against service level agreements, and supportive of the comments of David Bell, the senior managers of public service organisations report a greater level of accomplishment than do the managers from companies from the other sectors. In the other aspects of managing the outsourcing process, comparable standards of skills are reported. The capability to select appropriate service providers is viewed as acceptable and of comparable standard across the sectors. Likewise, the ability to concurrently manage a variety of outsourcing arrangements is reported as being of an acceptable and equal standard

Table 5.5 Managing transactional outsourcing: sector comparison

Capability	Sector		
Process management	Public services	Professional services	Manufacturing, engineering, construction
Selection of service providers	✓✓	✓✓	✓✓
Managing varying outsource arrangements	✓✓	✓✓	✓✓
Benchmarking service level agreements	✓	✓	✓
Monitoring performance against service level agreements	✓✓✓	✓✓	✓✓
Managing the transfer of resources	✓✓	✓✓	✓✓
Capturing previous outsource experiences	✓✓	✓✓	✓✓

Note: ✓✓✓ – well prepared; ✓✓ – prepared; ✓ – poorly prepared.

across the organisations involved in this study. Managing the transfer of resources to service providers with minimum disruption to the host organisation and capturing the learning gained from each outsourcing contract are also considered as being of an acceptable level across the sectors.

> Partnership has a number of characteristics. We envisage a Partnership Board to lead the strategy ... The Partnership Board ... would agree the business case around key investment decisions as well as ensuring that the partnership is working according to the performance standards it has been set. It will ensure that it pursues research and development regarding new developments, say in IT. It will also, in a sense, act as a forum for trying to sort out, at the highest level, any difficulties with the partnership – David Bell, CEO, Bedfordshire County Council, UK

David Bell promotes a partnership approach to developing relationships with suppliers and in so doing improving standards of quality of service. Similar comparable levels of performance are identified when examining the levels capability for effectively managing relationships with key suppliers (Table 5.6). The survey results show a high level of managerial capability across the sectors in relationship management skills. Such capability is reflected in the positive relationships and level of a shared understanding that is reported between partners. In fact, professional

Table 5.6   Managing supplier relations: sector comparison

Capability	Sector		
Supplier relations	Public services	Professional services	Manufacturing, engineering, construction
Shared understanding between partners	✓✓✓	✓✓✓	✓✓✓
Cultural match between partners	✓✓	✓✓✓	✓✓
Relationship management skills	✓✓✓	✓✓✓	✓✓✓
Managing changes in contractual obligations	✓✓✓	✓✓	✓✓
Consortium management skills	✓✓	✓	✓

Note: ✓✓✓ – well prepared; ✓✓ – prepared; ✓ – poorly prepared.

services organisations indicate they are more accomplished at creating an environment where an acceptable cultural match between partners can emerge. Public service organisations also display a greater capability in managing changes in contractual obligations that arise from having to respond to unexpected contingencies in the outsourcing programme. As David Bell indicates, public service managers report greater accomplishment at managing consortia type relationships, which managers from across the other sectors report as problematic for their organisation.

Considerable differences in managerial capability emerge concerning staff motivation and performance (Table 5.7). The motivation of staff involved in outsourcing programmes to continue to perform to high standards is low across all the sectors. Professional service organisations highlight that they have a more motivated workforce, whereas public service organisations emphasise low levels of staff motivation as do companies from the manufacturing, engineering and construction sectors. Further, public service organisations report lower levels of motivation amongst their managers than do companies in professional services, manufacturing, engineering and construction. The lower motivated public service managers are considered as not giving sufficient attention to motivating employees to improve their performance. Companies in professional services, manufacturing, engineering and construction report that greater attention is given by their managers to motivating employees. Such differences of attention to staff become apparent in that public service organisation indicate that they are less successful at improving the levels of performance of their employees.

Table 5.7 Managing internal relations: sector comparison

Capability	Sector		
Staff motivation and performance	**Public services**	**Professional services**	**Manufacturing, engineering, construction**
Motivating staff	✓	✓✓	✓
Motivated management	✓✓	✓✓✓	✓✓✓
Improving employee performance levels	✓	✓✓	✓✓

Note: ✓✓✓ – well prepared; ✓✓ – prepared; ✓ – poorly prepared.

Overall, the survey indicates that public service managers are more attentive to, and are well prepared for, managing the explicit transactional elements of outsourcing projects than are managers of professional services organisations and of manufacturing, engineering and construction companies. These results and the comments made by David Bell contradict the outcomes of inspections conducted by the US General Accounting Office in 1997, which concluded that US Government organisations were weak in monitoring and managing outsourcing contracts owing to poor levels of skills and capabilities in these areas. The investigation found that performance monitoring was the weakest link in the US Government's privatisation process because of the lack of skilled personnel. In contrast, the Kakabadse survey results indicate a change from four years ago, in that public service managers now display higher levels of skill in the transactional management of outsourcing contracts.

Impact of outsourcing

Despite the reported higher levels of operational skills in the transactional management of outsourcing contracts, senior managers of public service managers are more of the view that their organisations have not benefited from outsourcing (Table 5.8). As shown in Tables 5.4, 5.5 and 5.6, managers of public service organisations are rated as being equally operationally effective in administering outsourcing arrangements and also as being equally capable of benchmarking against known sector quality standards, as managers of companies from the other sectors. Where differences arise is in senior managers of public service organisations reaching a shared view concerning the value that has been gained through outsourcing (Figure 5.2) and on the increase in organisational effectiveness as a result of outsourcing (Table 5.8). Senior public service

Table 5.8   Enhancement through outsourcing: sector comparison

Capability	Sector		
Organisational enhancement	Public services	Professional services	Manufacturing, engineering, construction
Service/Product/process gain through outsourcing	✓	✓✓✓	✓✓

Note: ✓✓✓ – well prepared; ✓✓ – prepared; ✓ – poorly prepared.

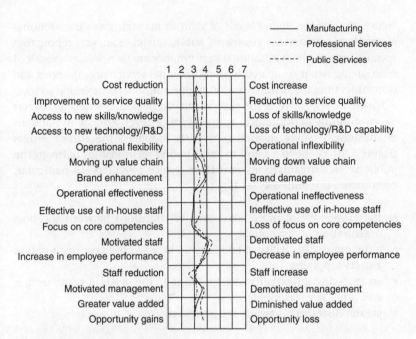

Figure 5.9 Outsourcing outcomes.

managers report that outsourcing has not contributed to making their organisation more effective in meeting goals, improving quality of service delivery or value for money.

A more detailed analysis shows the specific outcomes which public service managers consider to have been undermined by outsourcing (Figure 5.9). When compared to the views of managers from professional service organisations and manufacturing, engineering and construction companies, public service managers report that outsourcing has led to:

- reductions in service quality;
- loss of knowledge and skills in providing for particular services;
- less operational flexibility;
- less operational effectiveness;
- poor use of in-house staff;
- more demotivated staff;
- greater numbers of staff reductions;
- greater opportunity losses in terms of recognising and appropriately addressing internal organisation needs and in meeting community needs.

Hence, despite the higher levels of skills in managing the transactional elements of outsourcing contracts, public service managers report that specific aspects of organisational performance are impaired as a result of outsourcing when compared with professional service organisations and companies from the manufacturing, engineering and construction sectors.

Further, irrespective of the skills displayed by public service managers in monitoring performance against service level agreements and in establishing positive relationships with suppliers, the survey results (Figure 5.10) point to a trend towards poorer relationships between the public service organisations and their service providers. In particular, outsourcing is reported as leading to:

- the emergence of more adversarial relationships between the host organisation and suppliers;
- a decline in the quality of relationship between the host organisation and its suppliers;
- an emerging inflexibility in responding to the needs of communities and other key stakeholders;
- greater disrespect between the partners.

Overall, the relationship between public service organisations and their outsource service providers are reported as becoming more distant, which is damaging to meet agreed standards of service.

In effect, public service managers are identified as operationally skillful but strategically divided. The concerns raised by other writers and researchers in the strategy/policy arena concerning the negative impact of privatisation and outsourcing are supported by the Kakabadse survey

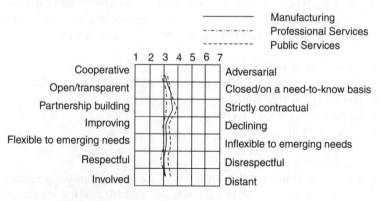

Figure 5.10   Quality of sourcing relationship(s).

and by the views of Alun Cole. The survey raises no doubts about the sense of responsibility of public service managers to their communities. In fact, it is considered that the managers of the public service display high levels of integrity concerning the quality of service for which they are accountable. However, the results do emphasise that public service managers feel that accountability to the public has been undermined by the disruption that arises from what they consider as the unnecessary outsourcing of various processes and activities which, though not critical, still have a powerful impact on the functioning of the host organisation. Other studies and reports support the views of the Kakabadse survey participants. The Department of Immigration and Multi-Cultural Affairs (DIMA), Australian Federal Government, for example, has highlighted that the outsourcing vendor was costing the department more than the cost of maintaining services in-house. Approximately 10 per cent of contracted service outcomes (i.e. service level agreements) were allegedly not delivered to standard, resulting in financial penalties being imposed on the vendor. Similarly, the UK's Ministry of Defence outsourced Helicopter Training required the service provider to purchase 38 helicopters that were attached to the training activity. The costs associated with this arrangement reduced the number of service providers who applied to take charge of the training services.

Summary

- Writers, researchers and government enquiries promote the view that as a result of technological advancement and the drive for value for money, outsourcing is considered a key strategic tool for enhancing organisational effectiveness in public service organisations.
- An examination of trends over the last 15 years emphasises that public service organisations have both adopted private sector management techniques and benchmarked themselves against private sector enterprise performance standards.

The Kakabadse survey

- Public service managers emerge as having comparatively less influence on the purchase of outsourcing services.
- Substantial differences of view are expressed by managers of public service organisations as to the value their organisation has gained from outsourcing.
- Greater use is made of the large international IT service providers by public services organisations than by organisations in the private sector.

- Basic services, IT services and facilities management are the key activities and processes being outsourced by public service organisations.
- Contrasting reasons for outsourcing exist. The two most frequently cited are to achieve best practice and to promote greater cost discipline and control over the management of public service organisations.
- In contrast to organisations from other sectors, outsourcing is viewed as non-critical to the current and future functioning of the organisation, but is recognised as affecting the manner in which the organisation operates.
- Managers of public service organisations are identified as highly capable in managing the contractual and transactional elements of outsourcing, as well as skilled in developing positive relationships with suppliers.
- Managers of public service organisations are considered as less able to motivate and improve the performance of their employees than managers of professional services and manufacturing, engineering and construction companies.
- The lack of shared view concerning the value to be gained from outsourcing by public service managers is considered to be jeopardising the prospect of further outsourcing.
- Outsourcing is considered as having a negative impact on the functioning of public service organisations.
- Managers of public service organisations consider that the decisions to outsource are not made in the best interests of their organisation.
- The quality of relationship between public service organisations and their suppliers are reported as declining.

References and further reading

For further information on developments in the philosophy and practice of the management of public service organisations, read Hogwood (1995), Dicken (1992), Boston (1995), Digings (1991), Korac-Kakabadse and Korac-Kakabadse (1997), Savas (1997) and Walsh (1991; 1995).

For an understanding of the impact of IT advances on the management of public service organisations, read Henderson and Venkatraman (1994), Korac-Boisvert and Kouzmin (1994a; 1994b), Halachmi and Montgomery (2000), Lavelle, Kramwiede and Sheu (2000) and Szymanski (1996) for the study of outsourcing in English local authorities.

For further reading on the DIMA case (Australia) of not meeting service level agreements, read Lundy (1999). For further information on the case of the UK's Ministry of Defence outsourcing of helicopter training, read Domberger (1998).

For the privatisation and outsourcing of public service activities, read Macgregor, Peterson and Schuftan (1998), Osborne and Gaebler (1992), Dodgson (1991;

2000), Australia Management Advisory Board (1992), Australia Commonwealth Government Report (1994; 1995), The European Council Report (1994), Sweden Prime Minister's Office Report (1994), Danish Ministry of Research (1994), OECD Best Practice Guide for Contracting Government Services (1997), Australia Industry Commission (1996), Outsourcing Government.com (2000), US General Accounting Office Report (1997), Treasury Board of Canada (1994) – Canadian Government Enquiry Report, USA National Performance Review (1993), USA State of California, – Task Force on Government Technology and Procurement (1994), ITNet (1999), Audit Commission (2000), HM's Treasury Guidance on Appraisal and Evaluation in Central Government (1997), UK Cabinet Office (1996), Government Information and Communication Services (GICS) UK (2000).

6
The New Entrants

Challenges for application service providers – the ASPs

Interview with David Mills, Vice President Commercial, FutureLink, Europe Ltd

---

Q: Which organisations come to you?

Mills: What we look for is what we call an applications break, moving
        from a smaller to a bigger application ... The second is where
        they (the users) have IT retention problems ... IT has got so
        big now that I need dedicated resources, then suddenly that's
        another reason to come to us ... the third reason is ... A look
        to other solutions!

Q: What type of company comes to you?

Mills: There is an accountancy company that we are working with ...
        And what you find is that IT sits either on the Operations
        Director or the Finance Director and he is doing it on a part-
        time basis with help from some others in the organisation. He
        may well be looking after the server at the weekend ... but
        they get to a point where they can no longer cope as these
        people do not have an IT department per se. For companies
        that do have an IT department, they have people employed
        at help desks, they have high-level specialists and when they
        start talking to an ASP, all their headaches go away and what
        we end up being is an additional project management
        resource for that IT department ... We can offer scalability for
        the business and budget predictability.

Q: How much customisation are you prepared to do?

Mills: Either running from the customer's site or we engage a chan-
        nel partner to do it for us ... For Seebrooks, we are running
        five applications that they have written in-house ... Dominoes
        (Dominoes Pizza) was about growth, focusing on their core
        business, predictability and scalability ... The Housing
        Corporation was a different set of drivers ... The Housing
        Corporation is a government body that hands out grants to
        house people. The value that we added to them was literally
        that we took their in-house applications on our data centre.
        What we did was enable 2400 users from different locations
        through the web.

Q: What about security? People do not like to part with their
        customer database finances. How do you overcome that?

Mills: I think security is in three areas. Physical security (location),
        viruses and psychological security. Psychological security is
        about making me (the user) feel comfortable because you
        understand my business. If my data centre crashes (users
        data centre) and you reload my profile, how do I know
        you're not going to reload my profile to my competitors ...
        So, we actually say – 'see that server, that's yours! See that
        hard disc drive that's running in that server, that's your hard
        disc drive.'

David Mills, a top manager at one of the more innovative and exciting
ASPs of today, FutureLink, highlights certain key challenges and concerns facing ASPs and their clients such as, the prime purpose of ASPs,
issues around customer profiling, degree of customisation and security.
Meeting these challenges is foremost in FutureLink's mind, as this
organisation is concerned not only with its growth and reputation,
particularly as it has operations in the USA, Canada and Europe, but
also with its service quality capability as it delivers Microsoft Exchange
and office services and is currently undergoing the Microsoft ASP
Certification programme. An additional stimulus to succeed is that
Microsoft is also an investor in FutureLink.

The issues surfaced by David Mills of quality and range of service
provision, adapting to customer needs and data security form integral
elements of this chapter. Specifically, the nature of ASPs and their history
are discussed. The different forms of application afforded by ASPs, and

the range of providers currently in the market place, are also analysed. The views of other writers concerning the benefits to be gained from ASPs, the challenges they face in terms of growth and survival and considerations for users of ASPs, form a further substantial element of this chapter. In contrast to the views emerging from the literature, the Kakabadse survey of ASPs indicates that many users are well satisfied with the service they receive and the number of ASPs who have become profitable is higher than expected. Finally, the chapter concludes by undertaking a brief analysis of two types of ASP, a stand-alone new entrant, Pragmatas, searching for their first client, and a network of ASPs clustered around a powerful vendor, namely Microsoft, the Microsoft ASP Forum.

Trends from the literature

Businesses and academic writers are beginning to recognise that businesses, and in particularly e-business enterprises, are no longer seeking specific technology fixes. Instead, private sector organisations are concerned with installing end-to-end e-business solutions that can transform their business model, enabling them to compete in the fast developing digital economy. As a result, enterprises are enhancing their internet strategy and related technologies by outsourcing particular information systems (IS) activities. Organisations are aligning themselves with business partners who offer a range of IS services on the basis that such services are performed more efficiently outside the host organisation. These relationships are forged in the belief that they enable the enterprise to focus on its core competences and the fundamental drivers of the business – its products/services, brands and customers. In response, and to better serve client needs, e-business architects are expanding their hosted or outsourced services far beyond any technology platform to incorporate business strategy and industry expertise. The emerging practice is that both established and emerging organisations are partnering with ASPs to manage the technology related aspects of their business. Many companies are already using ASPs to provide for their routine or packaged (predeveloped, solution-based software, normally available for use via licensing) products. The services and products provided range from Microsoft at the one end, through to Web hosting and the large and critical applications such as enterprise resource planning (ERP) and risk analysis applications, at the other. In effect, customer organisations have a choice between purchasing, implementing and maintaining packaged application software, such as Microsoft office, SAP, Oracle, Fanatical, Peoplesoft, and renting a general or customised form of the software through an ASP.

Organisations are no longer just procuring IT products. Rather they are buying e-services or selecting a 'one-stop shop' solution that will unburden them of the routine of purchasing, hosting and configuring well established software packages. Therefore, business organisations are shifting their attention from technology to understanding how to choose and manage the partners that will provide appropriate IT services that will enhance the organisation's growth, value and profitability. The few businesses and academic writers who have studied ASPs agree that the shift is from IT self sufficiency by the host organisation to the provision of comprehensive and continuous IS support.

A history of ASPs

The concept of an ASP can be tracked back to the 1960s practice of computing time-sharing, when expensive main frame computers and software applications were rented out on a time-sharing basis. Providers of these services were running an IT services bureau, as typified by the Payroll Bureau Service offered by Ross Perot's Electronic Data System to Fonto Lay, Blue Cross and other organisations. At the same time, the idea of Mulit's, a large scale computer system connected by telephone wires to terminals in offices and homes throughout a city, on a time share operating system, running continuously through a vast file of shared programmes and data was conceived by a group of engineers from the Massachusetts Institute of Technology (MIT) and from General Electric (GE) in 1963, though it was never put into practice.

These early attempts towards networked integration and with the decline in hardware and software costs, provoked businesses in almost every industry to question whether their need to maintain full scale applications for computer/networking support. By the 1980s technological advances and improved robustness in client/server and other component technologies, increased the uptake of internet and web-based applications to the point where the internet has now become the largest data and computing service delivery infrastructure. Thus a new platform has emerged for network-centric computing. Component technologies have made it possible to produce a number of reliable, distributed software applications that can be hosted (i.e. housed and run) geographically distant from the users, thus enabling greater specialisation and economies of scale. Hence, the separation of IT resources such as hardware, networks and software application, from information services, has led to the emergence of ASPs, firms that provide hosting and access to predominantly packaged software and associated services by a third party, and on a rental basis.

The principle of separating IT resources from computer services is not new. Parallels can be found in the public utilities such as electricity and gas. With electricity, for example, electrical power is the prime resource. Electrical application devices such as light bulbs and other equipment (heaters, stoves) transform electrical resource into light and heat. Those who provide the resource have no need to manufacture and offer electrical hardware as well. To do so would go against the common sense of specialisation and economies of scale. Similarly, the manufacture of computer hardware produces computing resources in the form of processor time, data and data-access bandwidth. Applications software consumes these resources and delivers services to users. Through rapid developments in server-based software embodied in web pages, users can utilise services by accessing data stored on remote servers (data centres) or running applications that are hosted on remote servers by using the internet as an 'extension card' between the machine (hardware) and the users input/output devices such as terminals and printers. As processing time cannot easily be delivered on a network, computing applications are usually hosted on servers, namely machines with high processing capabilities. Through not owning the servers and a range of computer applications, users are liberated from the ownership and management of such resources in exchange for payment for services delivered on a pay as you go basis. Thus ASP service providers offer enterprise level software and, in turn, charge customers a monthly per-use fee, which includes all installation, upgrade and maintenance, just as in other utility-based services. Hence, the emergence of utility-based computing through rental-based sourcing.

At the time of writing, there are approximately 700 ASPs in the USA and just over two dozen in the UK. The Gartner Group estimates that the size of the ASP market world-wide in 2001 stands at US$3.5 billion and will rise to US$25 billion by 2004. Some believe that the year 2001 will be the time when the ASP enterprise will 'cross the chasm' in the USA and begin to emerge as a mass market phenomenon. However, the few available trends for Europe highlight low revenues and few customers for European ASPs. Further, certain of the latest European Union (EU) reports indicate that small- and medium-sized enterprises (SME) with fewer than 49 employees represent 99 per cent of ASP customers and 37 per cent of ASP revenues. As SMEs do not have the capital to purchase the latest software and related technologies, the idea of utility rental solutions, with costs of service known in advance, appeals strongly.

Who are the ASPs?

In a narrow sense, ASPs refer to any third party whose main business is providing a software-based service to multiple customers over a wide area public and/or private network, such as the internet or wireless, in return for payment. In turn, service purchasers gain access to enterprise applications ranging from functionally oriented applications in the form of accounting and HR to generic applications in the form of commerce and customer services.

In its broader sense a variety of service providers fit the ASP category, such as management service providers (MSPs), network service providers (NSPs), storage service providers (SSPs), enterprise application service providers (EASPs) and other application service providers. All are able to deliver service over the internet which can be supported by a dedicated leased line, virtual private network or wireless technology. However, all offer an externally managed service, where the product (hardware or/and software) is owned/leased and managed remotely at the providers facility, allowing the service provider to centralise that service, thus enhancing scale economies. The ASP model provides one-to-many services, usually through standardised offerings to many clients, or customised offerings to a group of clients in particular markets, such as for government or the financial sector. Another feature of ASPs is the service-based fee structure run on an annuity-pricing model, per transaction or per-user. Payment is over time rather than up-front or balloon-style payments.

The common elements of ASP offerings are to provide a network communication service, systems infrastructure, a development environment, business applications, content and process support, process execution and consultancy. Many suppliers offer all or some of these.

With these service provisions in mind, currently, four generic models of ASP sourcing exist, namely:

- websourcing (or browser-based computing or web-based computing);
- wireless sourcing;
- application hosting;
- application outsourcing.

Websourcing

One thing is for sure. The web content, data application and then voice and video are all divergents. They are all going to come together. So you will be going to a web port to get access to your video, your voice, web content, everything. As that slowly starts to come, the number of subsidiaries is going to grow exponentially – Eamus Halpin, Group Chief Executive Officer, iRevolution plc

For Eamus Halpin, the web is a critical area of growth for ASPs. Websourcing refers to the provision of services via the World Wide Web. Web-native applications imply that software and data exist on the web and generally require high-speed internet access. Websourcing started out as web sited internet destinations that offered only static content such as words and images, but then grew by providing applications that offer dynamic, interactive experiences or 'stickiness' that keeps users returning to the site. Moreover, as Eamus Halpin highlights, a new generation of software vendors are bringing their applications to market in the form of web-based services that can be accessed directly over the internet. Sophisticated online applications alongside relevant content from a web site, catering to the specific needs of special interest groups, is now available.

Websourcing service providers have created 'enterprise-level software' and usually charge customers a monthly per-user service fee, which includes all installation, upgrades and maintenance. There are a number of categories of providers, such as network-based applications, internet business services, vertical industry web sites, and internet market places. Increasingly, e-commerce businesses in addition to websourced applications offer ancillary services, such as logo design or printing though web sites.

Wireless sourcing

Wireless sourcing refers to services provided over the wireless web usually to mobile devices, such as cellular phones and hand-held devices. Currently wireless or mobile commerce applications are extensions of web-based e-commerce solutions. Since users typically pay airtime for wireless web use, they are unlikely to spend time browsing or tolerate banner advertisements or other 'distracting' messaging without their permission. Hence, the 'wireline' web and 'wireless' web have to use a different development language. The wireline web employs hypertext mark-up language (HTML) technology, while the wireless web uses two development languages, hand-held device mark-up language (HDML) and wireless mark-up language (WML). These languages are accessed with different forms of browsers installed on mobile phones and other hand-held devices. According to McKinsey & Co, by 2003 e-commerce through mobile devices will have reached trading levels of between £10 billion and $15 billion world-wide. In turn, the Gartner Group predict that 40 per cent of business to consumers (B2C) e-commerce will occur through wireless connections. The basis on which such predictions are made is that although currently wireless web application mobility fills the gap due to PC unavailability, it is expected that within a few years wireless sourcing will have overtaken PC based applications. In fact, certain e-commerce players, such as Amazon.com and Yahoo, are already offering a mobile option.

Application hosting

Application hosting is the most common form of sourcing via ASPs. Despite the fact that the Internet industry uses the term application hosting, the difference from other forms of application services is only nominal. Several distinct sub-categories of application hosts exist, namely, internet web servers, application server hosts, e-business services, and internet based infrastructure services. The ISPs are the pioneers of the ASPs, in that the provision of hosted mail and web services is an application service. For example, if, an enterprise desires a web site but does not own a web server, then it is likely to use an ISP to host its web site. However, over time, the ISP industry has divided between those who provide access and connective service, and those who offer hosting services. These who offer hosting services have been joined by a new class of ASPs, which use the hosted model to provide internet-based applications and service. Those enterprises who offer a hosting service for sophisticated e-commerce, messaging, and other complex web hosting applications are, effectively, ASPs. An example of an application hosting ASP is TalkingNetsm, which has adopted a wholesale telephony application service provider model, and employs a soft-switch network to deliver carrier-class voice-over applications to data services providers. Talking-Netsm offers solutions for traditional data service providers that want to add voice to their portfolio but face several constraints, including regulatory hurdles, lack of in-house telephony expertise and capital limitations.

Application outsourcing

The actual cost of application software represents less than a third of the total cost of installation and maintenance. The necessary hardware, network access, support personnel, and other related activities and services are easily the largest part of an application's total cost of service. For example, the implementation of large-scale applications, such as SAP R/3 implementations, often run into the tens of millions of dollars thus leaving the way clear for an outsourcing option. Yet, unlike past deals, instead of handing over the complete IT infrastructure to an outside provider, organisations have selectively outsourced specific parts of their IT infrastructure, ranging from data networks to applications management, thus following the trend towards a fixed per-user price in the form of monthly subscription.

The most popular ASP applications being outsourced are ERPs, where the goal is to integrate the company's functional databases into a single computer system. According to a Conference Board survey (USA) from 117 firms spanning 17 countries, 87 per cent of the sample have adopted an ERP system. Companies are increasingly looking to intermediaries to be hosts of ERP functionality and as a result, most ERP software companies are offering an ASP option, either directly or in partnership. In turn, many ASPs have targeted companies of different sizes who may be able to take advantage of ERPs. In addition to the larger organisation, the aim is service smaller companies where extensive installation costs are not feasible. For example, in the USA within the wholesale sector, Prophet 21 has introduced an ASP option and for a flat monthly fee, its partner, Sales Systems, provides system administration and a complete and secure infrastructure with a predictable and economical cost to Prophet 21 customers. Customers enjoy a cost-effective alternative to internal information systems maintenance without incurring significant hardware, software or implementation investments.

Vendors also believe that over time, they will sell much of their hardware to service providers, as ASPs and ISPs. In effect, there will occur a shift in buying power from customers to ASPs, as end-users purchasing IT services will not care whose products are running their leased IS services. However, until that ostensible shift occurs, many ASPs may need the investment strength and, or, the brand recognition support of high profile vendors, as captured by the Microsoft Forum case study, later in this chapter.

Who are ASP providers?

The range of ASPs providers is growing rapidly and involves:

- start-ups/dot-coms;
- systems/software integrators;

- infrastructure providers;
- solution providers;
- network services or bandwidth and hosting providers (e.g. AT&T, MCI, Sprint and Bell);
- wireless application service providers (WASPs) (e.g. GoAmerica, Genie),
- software/hardware vendors (e.g. IBM, Mircrosoft, Oracle, PeopleSoft, SAP).

Start-ups

The range of start up enterprises of varying technical functionality and expertise, is extensive. However, the key question is their survival. According to the Gartner Group, by 2004 only 20 of the original current 480 ASP start-ups will remain. For example, Pandesic, the ASP formed by a joint venture between Intel Corporation and SAP AG, has already been an early casualty. Moreover in December 2000, KPMG Consulting Group sold its 49 per cent stake in ASP, Qwest Cyber.Solution LLC, which started in June 1999, back to its joint venture partner Qwest Communication International Inc., after Qwest Cyberland lost $65 million. Start-up ASPs seem to have created an image of expertise, but are emerging as a modern version of the Trojan horse. Initial clients are often provided by the venture capitalists that have interests in both the ASP and the client. And those ASPs that become successful they also are take-over targets as the market matures. Like so many other start ups, the success of many depends on the quality of their business plan, their 'public offering' and/or ultimate 'acquisition'.

Systems integrators

The ASP system integrators, or aggregators, promote a service of integrating a multiple and diverse group of hosted applications and then offering them to customers under one umbrella. Such services are mostly offered on a sign-on subscriber basis, through a single bill for all services. Some see aggregators as the way of the future, a one-stop shop for customers seeking a broad range of applications but providing a single point of contact to handle business relationships. The vertical focus of these firms seeks to maximise the value of the ASPs in-house industry specific expertise.

Network services, or bandwidth hosting providers

Bandwidth providers, who continue to see their profit margins under pressure from greater competition, are also jumping onto the ASP platform, where profit margins are much greater. Organisations like AT&T,

MCI, Sprint and Bell have either partnered with ASP service providers or are setting up their own ASP services. At the network layer sit the providers of basic communications, service centre resources and value adding information provider services (IPS). Providing communication services includes maintaining the physical connections, the routers that handle the IP traffic and the associated performance, reliability and security applications. Server centre resources typically provide collection space, protected electricity supplies and physical security and maintenance services. In contrast, value-adding IP services include virtual private networking (VPN), network chatting, streaming media, freeways and directory services.

Wireless application service providers (WASPs)

Currently, there are over 10 000 Wireless Application Protocol (WAP) sites in more than 95 countries. Further, a growing number of platforms can also be hosted by wireless information service providers (WISPs) such as GoAmerica, OminiSky Corp, Genie, the portal of BT Cellnet or GPRS and the Deutsche Telekom portal. The attraction of providing a myriad of services for all phones and other palm held devices, suggests an explosive growth for WASPs.

Solution providers

For many, academic and business writers alike, the solution providers are the true ASPs, who package the appropriate software and business professional services to create the complete service offering to end-users. A typical solution provider ASP, via an internet connection, provides client customised installations for virtually any application customers choose, often tailored to the particular needs of the business. Solution provider ASPs also offer local copies of the application, on-line or off-line. When subscribers are on-line, they are likely to receive features such as automated backups and the ability to access shared databases. Typically end-users will deal with only one provider, who will provide solutions for their customer as a result of entering into several commitments from different layers of providers. Within such layers may exist a provider who offers a contribution to a solution, but does not have a direct relationship with the end customer. This stratification results from multi-tiered architecture, performed on separate specialist servers, whereby each element of the solution can be catered for by separate specialist providers. At the other end, the end user experiences a seamless solution dealing with only one provider. Certain ASPs favour a vertically integrated model, whereby they own and control every element of the solution, thus achieving tighter integration and more assured control. Other ASPs promote the merits of outsourcing to best-of-breed providers and thus benefiting from greater economies of scale. Most ASPs outsource at least some elements of the customers desired solution to third parties.

Software/hardware vendors

Increasingly, hardware and software vendors are entering the field of application service provision. Many vendors and investors are realising that ASPs could represent a significant opportunity. Equally, they recognise that ASPs represent an emerging market, with unique customers, risks and challenges. In an effort to hedge potential losses and secure market share, mega-vendors from all IT areas, including IBM, Microsoft, Oracle, PeopleSoft, SAP, British Telecom, EMC, Sun, Dell and many others, have unveiled ASP migration programmes. These programmes are packages of services and products creatively designed to assist ASPs to enter the market to grow their businesses. In return, their loyalty is required in the form of exclusive agreements to build services using the vendor's technology (see the ASP Microsoft Forum case study at the end of this chapter). For example, IBM has launched a programme that assists IBM partners through the process of developing a business plan up to the actual launch of a new business or service. Such programmes are intended to encourage ASPs and application infrastructure providers (AIPs) to work together with the vendor's traditional partners who have established technical skills and, as such, act as a sales channel for both ASPs, independent software vendors (ISVs) and AIPs. In return for IBM's efforts, partners go through their programme and sign exclusive agreements to build services using IBM's technology. Similarly, in order to sell its dot-net strategy, Microsoft has created partnerships with ASPs who will in return exclusively use '.Net' server lines. Concurrent with such developments, vendors are also reshaping license agreements to exert more control over their product, so as to ensure that the customer receives effective service regardless of who provides the product.

Benefits of ASPs

The benefits to be gained from ASPs stem from the fact that software applications are distributed over multiple servers (dedicated machines) rather than dispersed over multiple 'clients' (individual PCs). Increased benefits are achievable from a combination of service rental models, component-based applications architecture and a computing environment for customers that is based on the 'fat server' and 'thin client' model. In effect, the bulk of data storage and processing is undertaken at the server end. On the basis that the responsibility for processing capability is transferred from customer to ASP, business and academic writers consider that the following benefits could be realised by purchasers, providers and investors who consider ASP sourcing.

Benefits for vendors and ASPs

- Eliminating distribution costs of software, manuals and stock keeping.
- No need for user installation requirements.
- Less illicit copying of software (software runs on the ASP server only).
- Instant and centralised upgrades of software for all subscribed customers (only at the ASP server).
- A one predicable/constant user base which leads to predicable cash-flows and revenue streams for ASPs.
- Ease of customer usage monitoring from a central point (at the ASP server).
- Continuously growing customer database.
- Potential for cross selling of services.
- Moving up the value chain towards higher-margin and less-competitive markets, as many core markets have come under pressure.
- Provision of standard offerings to achieve economies of scale for ASPs. Application of preconfigured, often industry specific templates is undertaken whenever possible. Moreover, ASPs identify which components of their product offerings can be reused across their client base and thus can be clear which part of their system they will or will not customise.
- Realising additional savings for ASPs through receiving discounts on software of around 30–40 per cent through resellers agreements with the vendor. ASPs have also attracted up to 40 per cent discounts on hardware components. Further, through using standardised offerings and preconfigured templates, ASPs can reduce up to 50 per cent, the cost and time of implementation of the application.
- Potential for attracting talent. By developing and investing in work routines and technical tools, ASPs can create an attractive working environment for ERP implementation and maintenance staff by leveraging their expertise over multiple customers.

Benefits for ASP subscribers

Financial benefits

- Restructuring the IT budget by changing to smaller monthly cash-outflows of a predictable nature presented by rental payment as an

alternative to up-front investments in infrastructure and implementation costs. Thus capital outflow (purchase of software infrastructure) is converted into operation outflow.
* Improved cost control. Service level agreements and predictable fixed charges provide control of user demands and considerably reduce overuse of IT/IS staff for unnecessary software changes.
* Capital expenditure is considerably reduced as there is no need for up-front capital expenditure for the purchasing of software and/or licensing or even application updates.

Business benefits

* Liberation from managing complex technology, regardless of the size or geographical location of the end user. The customer can focus on enhancing their core capabilities and running their business.
* Vertical market advantages can be realised through applications that support competitive advantage activities which can be safely sourced by the specialist ASP which understands that sector.
* The internet offers users greater choice through access to every rentable application via on-line availability.
* Enhanced benchmarking capability. ASPs service level agreements are easy to benchmark. As ASPs centrally support the software, methodology and databases needed to facilitate global benchmarking, the compilation of metrics and the analysis of best practices are fast adhering to standards needed to ensure quality benchmarking.
* Ease of a single supplier relationship interaction, irrespective of the chain and variety of supplying organisations in the background.
* Clear delineation of responsibilities amongst IT/IS suppliers. The client deals with only one supplier. The challenge of negotiating who is responsible for faults in the IT supply chain lies with the ASP.
* Accessibility of a seamless and real-time service from anywhere and any time.

Technical benefits

* Access to new technologies. Automatic updates of software are available immediately on the web site. ASPs upgrade complex systems, such as ERP, more efficiently and timely through the use of their industry specific, or functional, routines and templates.
* No software installation hassle. Once an agreement is signed, the software is ready to be used.

- No burden of software and hardware compatibility reconciliation issues.
- Rapid implementation of the selected system. Current implementation time frames are three months for a large-scale ERP system.
- Continuous access to technical expertise.
- Scalability of services. ASPs allow for ease of use of applications in the business portfolio. Customers can be of any size, from one user to an integrated delivery network. At minimum, a user needs only a PC with an internet or private network connection.
- Improved technical service and reduced downtime. The essence of ASPs is to provide a support service with sufficient expertise of a pre-dictable timely nature, sensitive to customer satisfactions level. Backed up by the software vendor's expertise, most on-line ASPs provide a support service 365 days a year, which is often higher than in-house services for most SMEs, or on par for corporate in-house services.
- Improved usage of existing in-house IS/IT staff, through releasing them to focus on new development work.
- Overcoming the problem of the IS/IT skills shortage. The need for technical support overheads, such as database and software adminis-trators and technical support staff, is eliminated.

As stated, effective ASP sourcing allows the end-user to focus on achieving their business objectives. Moreover, ASP sourcing can be achieved in a reasonable amount of time with costs that make sense thus allowing for greater business benefits. For an organisation that already has established IS/IT systems in-house, the reasons for undertaking ASP sourcing includes replacement of antiquated IT systems, standardising best practice or achieving specific business results. In contrast, SMEs have different reasons, for needing ASP services as they have minimal or no IS/IT systems in place, lack of available capital investment or lack of expertise.

Challenges facing ASPs

Six key challenges are identified in the literature as needing to be over-come if ASPs are to prove to be successful business ventures.

- *Architecture*. The architecture of applications for the delivery of IT services via the net has proved to be a challenge for the pioneering ASPs. Considering the short history of the internet and web-related technologies, most existing applications cannot easily migrate to the

ASP market as ASP hosting runs applications on a 'fat server' and 'thin client' basis, instead of the reverse. To fully benefit from the ASP layered infrastructure, ASP applications need to be designed to be run on component-based technologies. However, for those who believe that time-to-market is more important than quality of service, technologies exist that support a fast-tracking adaptation of existing client/server application for ASP hosting by logically extending the cord between the ASP server and client PCs' and other input/output devices. Although newly developed software will be designed for running on component technologies, given the current rate of investment within the IT industry and business, current applications may run for another 5–7 years, thus inhibiting the potential growth of ASPs.

- *Limited performance.* Performance limitations will persist due to the limited bandwidth of the internet. Bandwidth inefficiency is still likely to persist for the next 2–3 years. Network infrastructure limitations, slow rates of adoption, bottlenecks at the network peering nodes, and the disruption of the ongoing switching to fibre optic connections, will remain as challenges for the next 24 months.
- *Balance.* Achieving a balance between integration and customisation is demanding, as customisation can reduce economies of scale and hence profits. Therefore, maintaining sufficient constancy across clients to gain economies in the maintenance and support process, is important to achieve.
- *Reliability of support.* A reliable support structure can be expensive and difficult to engineer for new ASP market entrants. Most ASP service providers operate 24 hours a day, seven days a week endeavouring to offer 99.999 per cent availability, exceeding the average companies' internal experience of IS/IT support provision.
- *High start up costs.* The investment an ASP requires for the purchase and management of hardware, including servers, the data costs of storage and the managing of databases, operating systems and end-user applications, is prohibitive. Obtaining ownership of end-user software is also an expensive up-front cost. However, running licensed software and partnering with vendors can significantly reduce up-front costs, but such strategies also reduce margins, especially if multiple layers of suppliers are involved. Gross margins for ASPs in the United States typically range between 10–20 per cent of revenues, whilst in the software industry margins lie in the 80–95 per cent range. In the United Kingdom, typical ASP profit margins range between 15–20 per cent of revenues whilst in the software industry margins are higher in 60–80 per cent range.

- *Privacy*. Potential users of ASP services have repeatedly expressed concern concerning the privacy and security of their data. In response, ASPs are increasingly adopting 'military-grade network security' which in the future is likely to be considered the norm. Malicious server attacks in the form of viruses and deliberate overloading of servers, such as in year 2000 and the 'mafiaboy's' attack which paralysed key web servers in America by overloading the system through an exponential number of HTTP page requests, are unpreventable. Most web servers crash when their concurrent client connections exceed the capacity of their scalability.

In addition to closely interlinking with key vendors and in order to counter the significant investment and infrastructure challenges, numerous ASPs have become members of wide area networks which allow them to share information. Some have data synchronisation capabilities enabling them to service multiple offices. Synchronisation, however, tends to be complex to set up and maintain, and is the source of many support failures. Equally significant are the difficulties in hiring and keeping the skilled staff necessary to support an ASPs IT system. Such problems also face many dot-com companies, who end up using ASPs simply because they cannot hire sufficient competent IT people, thus inadvertently directing available labour more to ASP enterprises.

Considerations for purchasers of ASP services

To realise value from an ASP, academic and business writers consider the following questions as pertinent considerations for purchase and partnering:

- Does your sourcing strategy support the company's strategic proposition?
- Is it possible to clearly specify, through having relevant information for all system interfaces, what attributes of an ASP service are required?
- Does the capability exist to measure the effectiveness of the critical attributes of the service that is provided?
- Do you, as the management of the enterprise, recognising that there can be variation of supply, know what questions to ask so that corresponding adjustments in the system can be made?
- Is the technology solution needed, faster than in-house team(s) can build and/or adapt?

- What can your company afford – long-term capital outlay or fixed monthly payments?
- Is the level of service to be provided by the ASP more effective than in-house resources can provide?
- Have you, as the management, reviewed all available IT sourcing options?
- Is the particular ASP model/solution specific to your enterprise's industry and business model?
- Does the ASP model/solution offer a full suite of business applications?
- Does the favoured ASP exhibit staying power in the market place?
- Does the ASP in question customise applications that are unique to each users business and integrate its solutions with the user's legacy applications?
- Will the favoured ASP model provide for seamless integration with your enterprise's customers, suppliers and partners?
- Should a long-term contract with a proven partner be entered into when costs are likely to, initially, be high?
- Should a 'spot market' contract be adopted (a transaction for immediate delivery and payment), which is less expensive but could also offer less control?
- Can the provider be trusted with sensitive financial and customer information, offering the appropriate security, privacy, reliability and backup recovery?
- What are the risks, costs and benefits of an ASP sourcing option?
- Does the service contract agreement clearly specify who owns what data and that the ASP will not utilise that data other than for back-up and support purposes.

Academic and more popular business writers alike recognise that, as new market entrants, ASPs will need to prove themselves as reliable and effective service providers with staying power before they attract the larger corporate clients. In turn, the large corporations will have to reduce dependence on their IT departments in order to switch to sourcing their core applications via the internet. Within such an environment, various writers consider that ASPs will need to show a successful track record within the SME market before corporations decide to reduce their dependence on their complex IT departments.

It is expected that companies will gradually cull their way through available electronic services, experiment, evaluate and slowly but surely adopt new ways of IS/IT sourcing that will liberate their organisations from the complexity of machinery, cables and IT departments.

The Kakabadse survey

> ... Part of our philosophy is saying, 'right, you want to make money in the ASP space, brilliant, fantastic! You have got an application; a whole group of applications – even better. Bring your applications to us. We'll host them for you, give them back to you and let you run your ASP revenue stream by concentrating on selling your application, not managing it, but by breaking it into two components, the infrastructure and the delivery mechanism.' – Eamus Halpin, Group CEO, iRevolution plc

Through identifying one particular model of ASP, the networked enterprise, Eamus Halpin clarifies the benefits to be gained and the nature of the ASP service/purchaser relationship. In fact, from the ASPs that participated in the Kakabadse survey, four particular trends emerge:

1   The nature and profile of ASPs.
2   The nature and profile of users of ASPs.
3   Benefits to be gained from ASPs.
4   Nature of the ASP service/purchaser relationship.

ASP profile

In contrast to the current reports of academic and business writers, that profitability is difficult for ASPs to achieve, 44 per cent of the Kakabadse survey participants report profitability (Figure 6.1). Additionally, 14 per cent of ASPs in the sample indicate that being profitable is not due to sound vendor relationships but to the fact that their ASP activity is one small part of their total service offering.

Most ASP enterprises in the survey identify themselves as systems/ software integrators and as infrastructure providers (Figure 6.2). The second cluster of ASPs are identified as hardware vendors who provide ASP services and ASPs that are solution providers. The third cluster of ASPs are those that consider themselves to be management service providers, WASPs and network bandwidth and hosting providers. The Kakabadse survey results support existing trends that the greatest number of ASPs are systems/software integrators and solution providers.

The most commonly quoted service offered is application hosting, followed closely by application outsourcing and websourcing (Figure 6.3). Consultancy services in applications hosting, applications outsourcing and websourcing are also provided by certain ASPs. Additionally, the major

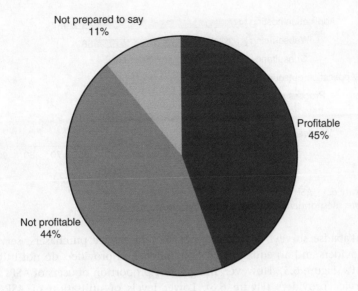

Figure 6.1 ASP profitability.

component technologies utilised by ASPs are Microsoft based, namely Microsoft.Net and Microsoft DNA (Figure 6.4). Enterprise JavaBean and CORBA are viewed as technologies considered appropriate for usage but currently not popularly adopted by the ASPs in the sample.

User profile

In keeping with the theme identified in the business and academic literature of current low usage of ASPs, a similar trend emerges from the

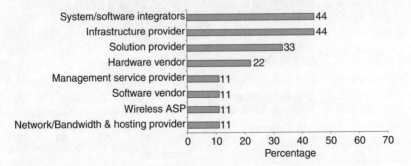

Figure 6.2 ASP description.
Note: Respondents selected multiple options.

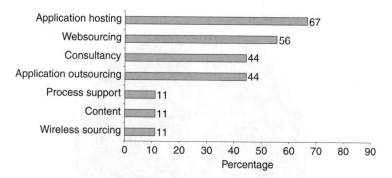

Figure 6.3   ASP service offering.
Note: Respondents selected multiple options.

Kakabadse survey. Eighty-four per cent of service purchasers, service providers and an equal mix of purchasers and providers do not utilise ASPs (Figure 6.5). However, the greatest proportion of users of ASPs are service providers (Figure 6.6). Lower levels of utilisation of ASPs is reported by those organisations that are a mix of purchasers and providers and those that are service purchasers. Such a finding supports trends discussed in the literature, namely, that considerable outsourcing is taking place between ASPs themselves. Differentation by type of ASP user most clearly emerges according to industry sector (Figure 6.7). Organisations that are primarily involved in supply chain management, logistics, procurement, and financial services emerge as the greater users of ASP services. Manufacturing, engineering and constructional companies

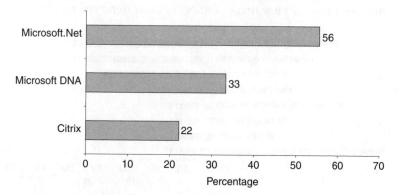

Figure 6.4   Major component technologies utilised.
Note: Respondents selected multiple options.

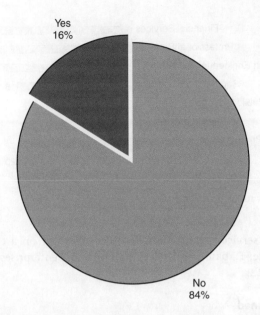

Figure 6.5 Proportion using ASPs.

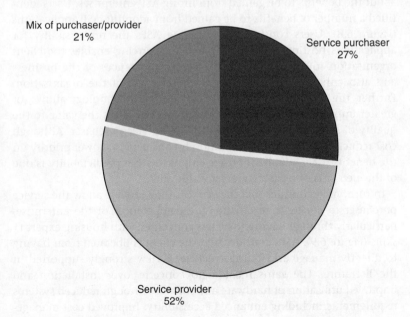

Figure 6.6 Type of end-user.

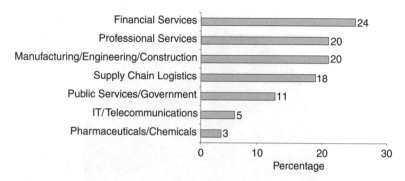

Figure 6.7   Industry sector of end-users.

and public service organisations also use ASPs but on a considerably smaller scale. IT based and telecommunication enterprises report low usage of ASPs.

Benefits gained

Both users of ASPs and the managers of ASP enterprises were asked about the benefits to be gained from hiring ASP enterprises. Users identified a number of benefits to be gained from adopting ASP applications (Figure 6.8). Users consider that offering ASPs the responsibility for applications hosting, websourcing and outsourcing enables the client organisation to focus more on the core competences of the business and also enhances the operational effectiveness of the organisation. Further, the access to new skills, knowledge and technology allows for greater improvements in service quality and enhances the value to the quality of services/products offered by the service purchaser. Although cost reduction through ASP utilisation is considered as lower priority on the benefits list, a number of users emphasise that predictability is one of the elements of realising greater 'value add'.

In turn, ASPs consider that the services they provide allow the service purchaser to concentrate on the core competences of the enterprise, particularly through having to be less concerned with housing expert IT skills (Figure 6.9). ASPs consider that the client is liberated from having to directly manage an IT infrastructure, a view strongly supported in the literature. The gains include no concerns over installation and improved utilisation of hardware and software through reduced systems requirements including enhanced accessibility. Improved cost management is placed high on the list of benefits to be gained by ASPs.

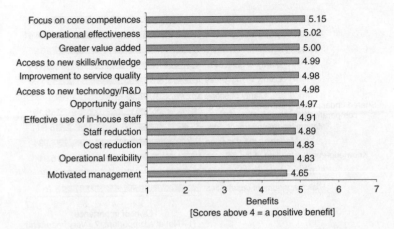

Figure 6.8 ASP benefits: end-users perceptions.

ASP service/purchaser relationship

Similar to the findings highlighted in Chapters 2 and 3, service purchasers identify 12 success factors critical to managing the ASP service/purchaser relationship effectively (Figure 6.10). The highest rated success factor in the ASP service/purchaser relationship is choice of partner. The second is in reaching agreement and clarity concerning the scope of each exercise. Clarity of objectives, clarity concerning expected outcomes and scope of work are almost as highly rated as the clarity of responsibilities that are expected to be fulfilled by the ASP. Managing the needs of customers

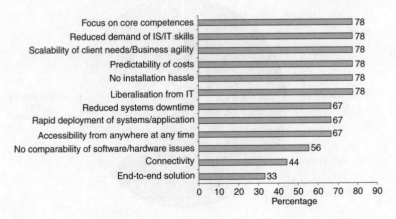

Figure 6.9 ASP benefits: ASPs perceptions.

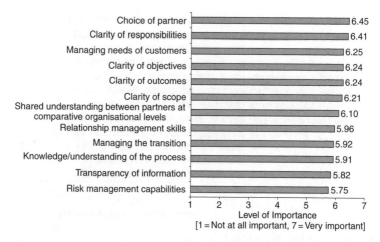

Figure 6.10   Critical success factors: end-users perceptions.

and relationship management skills also emerge as high on the list of
factors in the selection of an ASP and the sustainability of that relationship. Further, users highlight their positive experiences of ASPs (Figure
6.11). Sixty-four per cent of the sample indicate their satisfaction as a
result of having utilised ASPs. In particular, ASP providers are considered

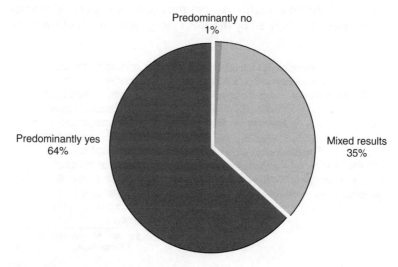

Figure 6.11   Successful outcomes using ASPs.

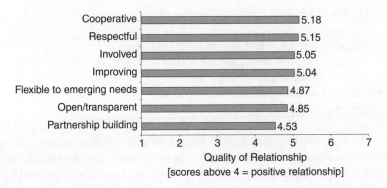

Figure 6.12 Quality of sourcing relationship: end-users perceptions.

as cooperative, respectful and fully involved with their clients (Figure 6.12). ASPs are also viewed as flexible in their response to emerging client needs and transparent in their dealings with service purchasers.

Case study: Pragmatas

Pragmatas is a new ASP market entrant, formed in the autumn of year 2000. Pragmatas provides an integrated HR service by modelling the HR process and by utilising GT-X technology to achieve substantial cost savings through introducing self-help HR without having to invest in new technology or database management. Through having created a nearly unique HR Life Cycle Model, Pragmatas considers that it is possible to quickly and clearly identify the client's HR needs and provide solutions appropriate to the client's expectations. The reason GT-X technology is favoured is that GT-X offers a two-way communication channel, in electronic dialogue, between databases, often written in different software, languages, that presumably existed in isolation on a client's corporate server(s). Through GT-X, Pragmatas offers a single point of entry for corporate clients databases relating to the HR function, without the need to invest in new database software. In effect, existing software packages can be maintained.

Crucial to the Pragmatas service offering is managers' assumption that the HR function is not delivering maximum value with maximum efficiency. An examination of the macro features inherent in the HR function reveal distinctive phases in the recruitment, employment and release of people, a life cycle with a beginning, an application and a natural ending.

The HR function is being challenged to:

- improve service to employees and managers;
- eliminate process steps, approvals and forms;
- reduce administrative costs;
- raise the profile of HR in strategic areas;
- increase information access.

The HR function, therefore, is viewed as a mix of strategy and policy setting, transactional administrative activities, human interaction and technology. The ideal HR function is where HR is predominately a strategic resource supported by a responsive transactional capability and also a system of easy access to information, delivered via a self-service application which uses a variety of technological advances.

The ideal HR function has the ability to:

- identify and understand the distinctive HR phases;
- define the key elements of policies and processes within each phase;
- rank the policies and processes in order of business benefit;
- highlight areas of organisational or work-flow complexity which are creating delivery problems;
- provide the opportunity for the introduction of best practice;
- determine the most appropriate solution (outsourcing, insourcing, web, self-service, call-centre) so as to gain greater business benefits and customer satisfaction.

Pragmatas emphasise that the HR Life Cycle Model helps produce these deliverables. An activity analysis of the HR function reveals five distinct phases. Each phase has both an input and an output element and numerous aspects within the phase that depend on the level of activity or focus required by the organisation.

The progressive nature of the phases, the impact and output associated with each phase and the key elements within each phase are outlined in Table 6.1.

The outline illustrates the 'individual' nature of each phase and the 'handover' points between phases. Within each phase are the elements, or steps that will normally be followed to complete a phase. Within each element, the HR contribution involves substantial transactional administration, employee access to information, technology and service delivery. The HR Life Cycle Model can show where companies can appropriately reduce the costs of their existing systems. The phases

Table 6.1 Pragmatas HR Life Cycle Model

Phase	Elements	Typical process examples
Pre-joining (decision to offer employment)	Need assessment	Business case, budget, job definition, candidate's profile
	Market position	Internal/external advertising, recruitment channels
	Recruitment and assessment	Application reviews, interviewing, profiling and assessment
Initial employment	Offer of employment	Preparation of employment
		Package, letter, terms, contract
	Reference checks	Medical security, qualifications, employer, personnel
	Pre-Day 1 requirements	Workplace location, Security, IT systems
	Commence employment	Data entry, induction, internal communication
Cultural framework (retaining employee until termination decision)	Compliance	Employment legislation, e.g. working hours, grievance handling, maternity, etc.
	Business order	Ethics, patents, confidentiality, information access, expenses, travel, etc.

Table 6.1 (continued)

Phase	Elements	Typical process examples
Ending employment (termination decision until employee leaves)	Strategy based retention	Compensation and benefits plans; performance management; overseas assignments, training and development
	Causes	Resignation, retirement, redundancy, dismissal, death, etc.
	Leaving action	Data entry, return of property, internal communication
	Employee specific	Claw-back provisions, loans, pensions, extended interview
	Redundancy specific	Consultation, notification, calculations
	Temporary ending	Leave of absence, short-term transfer
After employment (employee leaves and all enquiries and legislative requirements are satisfied)	References	Employment, Social Security, Security, Password
	Pension/insurance	Pensions Administration and Benefits; insurance-medical life
	Communication	Post-employment contact
	Employee archiving	Record retention for employment, tax
	Prebirth	Consultancy or contractor arrangements

where costs are a concern can be discovered and, through an analysis of the elements and processes, so can the areas for work flow improvement or the use of alternative methods.

When a company is considering outsourcing to replace or support the existing HR service, then the model can be used to determine the phase and/or processes where alternative sourcing would be appropriate. Examining the relevant data and work flow processes can provide the basis for the business case and also highlight the areas where linkage to other processes within the company is needed.

The Pragmatas HR Life Cycle Model is of value to companies wishing to automate transactional HR activities and provide self-service delivery via the latest technology options (be they GT-X or not). Since some key outcomes will include a quicker administration delivery service, increased customer satisfaction and substantial cost reduction, it is vital that companies adopt a disciplined analytical approach to determine the extent of the self-service solution.

Case study: Microsoft ASP Forum

> The four of us created it, out of a need to go to market for one of the Microsoft exhibitions... I think it is very important that we get the overall message out into the market place, backed by someone who has backed their entire future in the software and services arena, namely, Microsoft. More importantly, I think one of the biggest attributes that we could bring to this is really explaining in words of one syllable what .Net actually means, because for vendors and for end-users alike, they really do not have a clue – Eamus Halpin, Group CEO, iRevolution plc

The emergence of a cluster of ASPs around the Microsoft brand is a relatively new development. As Eamus Halpin points out, the pivotal point of the forum is Microsoft's .Net innovation, which Microsoft promote as beyond browsing and beyond dot-com. Microsoft are forging a new generation of software that attempts to integrate computing and communications in a manner that will offer IS developers the tools they require to transform the way they utilise the Web. The intent is that developers, businesses and consumers should be able to harness technology by shifting away from individual web sites connected to the internet through multiples of computers and other electronic devices and services, interconnect them and thus deliver for richer solutions. In effect, .Net services allow unrelated web sites to talk to one another. Users do not have to be inconvenienced by needing to open new programmes or even go to new web sites. Users will have greater control over the volume and quality of information that will reach them by ensuring that computers, other electronic devices and web sites collaborate with each other. The members of the ASP Forum identify the following advantages of pursuing membership:

- generating customer leads so that each member would leverage, to their advantage, such emerging relationships;
- promoting a common philosophy and approach amongst the members so as to promote a consistent image in the market place;
- generating a cohesive approach to sales and marketing so as to allow for greater penetration of an emerging but highly competitive market place;
- offering particular services and products and from that experience leveraging into different market areas;
- exploring amongst forum members how to improve the product and service provision so as to continually provide value to customers;
- promoting a meaningful market segmentation strategy through highlighting the key capabilities of the Forum;
- promoting economies of scale by generating desired but more standard development tools;
- leveraging the Microsoft brand;
- provide customers with alternative price structured packages for the provision of hardware and software services. Through maximising on economies of scale, a better deal can be offered to customers, in terms of cost effectiveness, through being able to share costs via better access to Microsoft products. Customers know how much they are going to spend every month;
- educating the market concerning the value to be gained from utilising the services of ASPs.

... the Forum believes that software as a service can help an organisation to maintain and increase profitability by supplying the technical expertise necessary for progression in today's market place, without taking resources away from core business activities. Service is still key and by talking to their customers ASP suppliers are now offering more tailored services and individual service level agreements – Martin Walker, Chair, Microsoft ASP Forum (Software as a Service)

The Microsoft ASP Forum is an interesting development. The service technology link outlined by Martin Walker is key to the survival and growth of this enterprise. The ultimate test of the Microsoft ASP Forum is level of membership. At the time of writing, the number of partners joining the Forum is increasing.

Summary

- The ASP market has only really been active since 1997.
- The ASP market provides for alternative IT sourcing arrangements, whereby the host organisation does not have to incur substantial capital investment in IT resources, does not have to hire well trained IS/IT personnel nor has to transfer existing IS/IT staff and managers to the supplier (see Table 6.2). The ASP supplier provides all the required hardware and software applications, their maintenance and upgrades on a rental basis. In this way, the host organisation is provided with greater predictability of costs and a one-stop-shop service.
- As the ASP market is new, it is predicted that a considerable number of ASPs will have a limited period of tenure due to their having to incur high up-front costs and/or their inability to effectively brand and market themselves.
- The term ASP covers a broad range of providers including MSPs, NSPs, SSPs and EASPs. These providers could be start-ups, dot-coms, systems/software integrators, infrastructure providers, solutions providers.
- The range of sourcing services include websourcing, wireless sourcing, application hosting, application outsourcing.

The Kakabadse survey results

- In contrast to the literature, the Kakabadse survey identifies a higher than expected number of ASPs as profitable.

Table 6.2 Outsourcing vs. ASP sourcing

Outsourcing	ASP Sourcing
Take over people	No take over of people
Customisation as necessary	Minimal customisation (if any)
Software belongs to host organisation	Application is rented
Investment in hardware/software infrastructure	Rental of services, including upgrades
Product orientation	Service orientation
High up-front costs/gains	Predictable costs

- Most ASPs are identified as systems/software integrators, infrastructure providers and solutions providers offering application hosting, websourcing, consultancy and application outsourcing services.
- Few organisations call upon the services of ASPs but of those that do the greater majority come from financial services, professional services, manufacturing, engineering and construction and supply chain/logistics.
- Both end-users and ASP enterprises concur as to the key benefits to be gained from utilising the services of ASPs.
- The majority of end-users consider ASPs as cooperative, respectful and involved with their customers.
- The majority of host organisations consider that successful outcomes have emerged from using ASPs.
- In order to survive, a growing number of ASPs are forming relationships with key vendors in order to leverage off the vendor's brand and channels to market and also to capitalise on greater economies of scale.

References and further reading

For further information on the emergence of ASPs, their history and the growing trend for rental-based sourcing read:

- for web-based applications, Barnet (2000).
- for partnering with the 'right' ASP, Cameron (2001).
- for the future growth of the ASP market, Whalen (2000), Paul (2001a, 2001b) and Taylor et al. (2001).
- for the different forms of applications, Bennett and Timbrell (2000) and Ebbsen (2000).
- on the history of ASPs, Christensen (2001), Marshall (2001) and Tao (2000).

For the further information concerning the different types of ASPs, read Naden (2000), Rysavy (2001), Whalen (2000), Duval (2000), Berry (2001), Ante and Borrus (2001), Tarode (2000), Paul (2001a; 2001b)), Follett (2001), Rooney (2001).

For an analysis of the benefits to be gained from utilising ASPs, read Wainewright (2000), Bennett and Timbrell (2000), Andreu and Ciborra (1996) and Naden (2000).

For an examination of the challenges facing ASPs and, as a result, the issues users should consider before hiring ASP services, read Whalen (2000), Tao (2000), Taylor et al. (2001), Kakabadse et al. (2000) and Christensen (2001). For further information on Microsoft's .Net strategy, read Microsoft.Net: Realising the Next Generation Internet (2000).

Bibliography

Agence France Presse (2000) 'EDS wins biggest government IT contract, hopes to expand', October 9, Washington.

Andreu, R. and Ciborra, C. (1996) 'Organisational learning and core capabilities development; The role of IT', *Journal of Strategic Information Systems*, 5(1): 111–27.

Ante, E. and Borrus, A. (2001) 'In search of the Net's next big thing', *Business Week*, March 26, pp. 60–61.

Alexander, M. and Young, D. (1996) 'Strategic outsourcing', *Long Range Planning*, 29(1): 116–19.

Aoki, M. and Dore, R. (eds) (1996) *The Japanese Firm: The Sources of Competitive Strength*, Oxford University Press, Oxford.

Asanuma, B. and Kikutani, T. (1992) 'Risk absorption in Japanese sub-contracting: a microeconomic study on the automobile industry', *Journal of Japanese and International Economics*, 6(1): 1–29.

Audit Commission (2000) Briefing, February 23, *http://www.audit-commission.gov. uk/ac2/BV/seeing.htm*

Australia, Commonwealth Government (CG) (1994) Working Nation: Policies and Programs, Presented by the Prime Minister, the Honourable P.J. Keating, House of Representatives, 4 May 1994.

Australia, Department of Employment, Education and Training (DEET) (1995) *Client First: The Challenge for Government Information Technology* (Report of the Minister for Finance), Information Technology Review, Canberra, March.

Australia, Management Advisory Board (MAB) (1992) *The Australian Public Service Reformed: An Evaluation of a Decade of Management Reform*, AGPS, Canberra, December.

Australian Industry Association (AIA) and the Department of Communications, Information and Technology and the Arts (DoCITA) (1999) *The IT Engine Room – A Report*, DoCITA, Canberra.

Bain, S. (2000) 'BoS outsources trustee services', *The Herald*, Glasgow, July 4, p. 18.

Barker, J. (1992) *Future Edge*, Morrow, New York.

Barnet, M.J. (2000) 'Benchmarking at its Best', *Strategic Finance*, 82(6): 58–63.

Bennett, C. and Timbrell, G.T. (2000) 'Application Service Providers: Will They Succeed?', *Information Systems Frontiers*, 2: 195–211.

Bensaou, M. (1999) 'Portfolios of buyer–supplier relationships', *Sloan Management Review*, 40(4) (Summer): 35–44.

Blumenstein, R. (1997) 'GM puts onus for some costs on suppliers', *The Wall Street Journal*, May 16, p. A3.

Boston, J. (ed.) (1995) *The State under Contract*, Bridget Williams, Wellington.

Bowen, W. (1984) 'The prospects for productivity', in Fortune Magazine Editors (eds), Working Smarter, Penguin Books, New York, pp. 1–121.

Brueck, F. (1995) 'Make versus buy: the wrong decision costs', *McKinsey Quarterly*, 1(1): 28–47.

Cameron, P. (2001) 'Slaying the competition dragon', *CMA Management*, 75(1) (March): 51–52.

Chalos, P. and Sung, J. (1998) 'Outsourcing decision and managerial incentives', *Decision Science*, 29(4) (Fall): 901–19.

Christian, N. (1997) 'Chrysler suppliers' cost saving ideas likely add $325 million to its 1997 net', *The Wall Street Journal*, June 5, p. A6.

Christensen, C.M. (2001) 'The Past and future of competitive advantage', *Sloan Management Review*, 42(2) (Winter): 105–9.

Cross, J. (1995) 'IT outsourcing: British Petroleum's competitive approach', *Harvard Business Review*, 73(3) (May–June): 94–102.

Currie, W. and Willcocks, L.P. (1997) *New Strategies in IT Outsourcing: Major Trends and Global Best Practice – Report*, Business Intelligence Ltd, London, December.

Cusumano, M.A. and Takeishi, A. (1991) 'Supplier relationships and management: a survey of Japanese transport and United-States auto plants', *Strategic Management Journal*, 12(8): 563–88.

Dataquest (1999) *Company Reports*, Dataquest, Gartner Group, Stamford.

Davidow, W.H. and Malone, M.S. (1992) *The Virtual Corporation*, Harper Business, New York.

Davidson, W. (1983) *The Amazing Race, Winning the Technorivalry with Japan*, John Wiley, New York.

Dicken, P. (1992) *Global Shift: The Internalization of Economic Activity*, PCP, London.

Digings, L. (1991) *Competitive Tendering and the European Communities*, Association of Metropolitan Authorities, London.

DiRomualdo, A. and Gurbaxani, V. (1998) 'Strategic intent for IT outsourcing', *Sloan Management Review*, 39(4) (Summer): 67–80.

Dodgson, M. (1991) 'The Future for Technological Collaboration', Emerging New International Technology Order: Opportunities and Challenges for Korea, STPI International Conference, 5 September, Seoul, Korea.

Dodgson, M. (2000) *The Management of Technological Innovation*, Oxford University Press, Oxford.

Domberger, S. (1998) *The Contracting Organization: A strategic Guide to Outsourcing*, Oxford University Press, Oxford.

Duval, M. (2000) 'ASPs: The Good, The Bad, The Ugly', Intractive Week, May 8, *http://www.zdnet.com/intweek/stories/news*

Dyer, J.F. and Ouchi, W.G. (1993) 'Japanese-style partnership: giving companies a competitive edge', *Sloan Management Review*, 35(1): 51–63.

Earl, M.J. (1996) 'The risks of outsourcing IT', *Sloan Management Review*, 37(3) (Spring): 26–33.

Ebbesen, A.M. (2000) *Western European Application Hosting 1999–2004 Markets and Trends – Software Vendor Perspective – IDC Report*, International Data Corporation (IDC), USA, June.

Finlay, P.N. and King, R.M. (1999) 'IT outsourcing: a research framework', *International Journal of Technology Management*, 17(1–2): 109–28.

Follett, J.H. (2001) 'Avenues to ASP aggregation', *Computer Reseller News*, Issues 929, January 22, pp. 73–74.

Foremski, T. (1999) '$150 bn market in sight', *Financial Times, FT-IT 2*, August 4, p. 2.

Foremski, T. (2000) 'Companies and finance: international: EDS wins Dollars 3.3 bn contract', *The Financial Times, USA Edition 2*, August 9, Wednesday, Companies & Finance: International, p. 17.

Forester Research Inc. (1999) *Outsourcing's Future – Report*, Forester Research Inc., Cambridge, April.

Forst, L.I. (1999) 'Outsourcing: You get what you ask for', *Journal of Business Strategy*, 20(1) (May/June): 11–14.

Gartner Group (1999) *The Changing External Services Market – Report*, June 30, No. Findg-19990630-01, Gartner IT Executive Program (gartner6.gartnerweb.com.).

Gibb, S. (2000) 'Evaluating HRM effectiveness: the stereotype connection', *Employee Relations*, 22(1): 58–75.

Government Information and Communication Services, UK (GICS) (2000) 'Why our work is different: Value for money', *http://www.cabinet-office.gov.uk/gics/why/money.htm*

Grant, R.M. (1995) *Contemporary Strategy Analysis*, Blackwell Business, Cambridge.

Halachmi, A. and Montgomery, V.L. (2000) 'Best value accountability: Issues and observations', *International Review of Administrative Sciences*, 66(3) (September): 387–414.

Hall, C. and Domberger, S. (1995) 'Competitive tendering for domestic services: a competitive study of three hospitals in New South Wales', in S. Domberger and C. Hall (eds), *The Contracting Casebook: Competitive Tendering in Action*, AGPS, Canberra, pp. 99–126.

Harrison, B.T. (1994) *Lean and Mean: The Changing Landscape of Corporate Power in the Age of Flexibility*, Basic Books, New York.

Heikkila, P. (2000) 'IBM scoops $2000 m outsourcing deal', *Procurement*, August 11, p. 1.

Hein, K. (1997) 'Reengineering undergoes reconstruction', *Incentive*, 171(2): 5.

Heller, R. (1996) 'Downsizing's other side', *Management Today*, March, p. 23.

Helper, S.R. and Sako, S. (1995) 'Supplier relationship in Japan and the United States: are they converging?' *Sloan Management Review*, 36(3): 77–84.

Henderson, J.C. and Venkatraman, N. (1994) 'Strategic alignment: A model for organisational transformation via information technology', in T.J. Allen and M.S. Scott-Morton, *Information Technology and the Corporation of the 1990s*, Oxford University Press, Oxford, pp. 202–20.

HM Treasury's (1997) Appraisal and Evaluation in Central Government, HMSO, London.

Hogwood, B. (1995) 'Public Policy', *Public Administration*, 73(1): 59–73.

Inkpen, A.C. and Beamish, P.W. (1997) 'Knowledge, bargaining power, and the instability of international joint ventures', *Academy of Management Review*, 22(1): 177–202.

International Data Corporation (IDC) (1999) Marphy, C., Ker, S. and Ross, L.M. (1999) *U.S. and Worldwide Outsourcing Markets and Trends, 1998–2003*, Report No. W19322, IDC, Framingham.

ITNet (1999) *Index: Looking into the Local Government Outsourcing Market*, ITNet Index, Birmingham.

Jaques, E. (1951) *The Changing Culture of the Factory*, Tavistock, London.

Jaques, E. (1979) *Taking Time Seriously in Evaluating Jobs*, Harvard Business Review, 57(5): 124–32.

Jones, C. (1994) 'Evaluating software outsourcing options', *Information Systems Management*, Fall, pp. 28–33.

Kakabadse, A.P. (1991) *The Wealth Creators: Top People, Top Teams and Executive Best Practise*, Kogan Page, London.

Kakabadse, A.P. (2000) From individual to team to cadre: tracking leadership for the third millennium, *Strategic Change*, 9(5): 5–16.

Kakabadse, A.P. (2001) *New Face in the Top Teams: how to ensure a good fit*, Financial Times: Mastering Management, Monday, January 15, pp. 8–10.

Kakabadse, A.P. and Kakabadse, N. (2000a) Sourcing: New Face to Economies of Scale and the Emergence of New Organisational Forms, *Knowledge and Process Management*, 7(2): 107–18.

Kakabadse, A.P. and Kakabadse, N. (2000b) Outsourcing: A Paradigm Shift, *Journal of Management Development*, 19(8) (Monograph): 668–778.

Kakabadse, A.P., Kakabadse, N. and Macaulay, S. (2000) Outsourcing: Current Future Practice', *Report for ISRC Members*, Cranfield School of Management, Cranfield, November.

Kakabadse, A.P. and Kakabadse, N. (1999) *Essence of Leadership*, International Thompson, London.

Kakabadse, A.P. and Myers, A. (1996) 'Boardroom skills for Europe', *European Management Journal*, 14(2): 189–200.

Kakabadse, A.P., Okazaki-Ward, L. and Myers, A. (1996) *Japanese Business Leaders*, International Thomson, Aldershot.

Kawasaki, S. and McMillan, J. (1987) 'The design of contracts: evidence from Japanese subcontracting', *Journal of Japanese and International Economics*, 1(3): 327–45.

Kay, J. (1993) *Foundations of Corporate Success*, Oxford University Press, Oxford.

Kessler, I., Coyle-Shaprio, J. and Purcell, J. (1999) 'Outsourcing and the employee perspective', *Human Resource Management Journal*, 9(2): 5–19.

Kliksberg, B. (2000) 'Rebuilding the state for social development: Towards "Smart Government"', *International Review of Administrative Sciences*, 66(2) (June): 241–57.

Kim, C.W. and Mauborgne, R. (1997) 'Value innovation: the strategic logic of high growth', *Harvard Business Review*, 75(1) (January–February): 40–8.

Klein, P. (1999) 'Outsourcing's third wave', *Information week*, Issue 761, Manhasset, November 15, pp. 126–7.

Korac-Boisvert, N. and Kouzmin, A. (1994a) 'Soft-Core Disasters: A Multiple Realities and Crisis Perspective on IT Development Failures', in H. Klages and Hill H. (eds), *Trends in Public Sector Renewal*, Peter Lang Publishing House, Berlin, pp. 71–114.

Korac-Boisvert, N. and Kouzmin, A. (1994b) 'The Dark Side of Info-Age Social Networks in Public Organisations and Creeping Crisis', *Administrative Theory and Praxis*, 16(1) (April): 57–82.

Korac-Kakabadse, A.P. and Korac-Kakabadse, N. (1997) *Leadership in Government: Study of the Australian Public Service*, Ashgate Publishing, Aldershot.

Korac-Kakabadse, A.P., Korac-Kakabadse, N. and Kouzmin, A. (1999) 'The changing nature of the social contract and the consequences', in Mazain Ahmed (ed.), *Public Service Management: Achieving Quality Performance in the 21st Century*, Eastern Regional Organisation for Public Administration (EROPA) and Public Service Department, Manila, pp. 450–72.

Kuhn, T. (1970) *The Structure of Scientific Revolutions*, University of Chicago Press, Chicago.

Kutnick, D. (1999) 'The externalisation Imperative', *CIO: The Magazine for Information Executives*, February, pp. 27–9.

Laabs, J. (1998) 'Why HR can't within today', *Workforce*, May, pp. 62–74.

Labib, N. and Appelbaum, S. (1993) 'Strategic downsizing: a human resources perspective', *Human Resource Planning*, 16(4): 69–91.

Lacity, M.C., Willcocks, L.P. and Feeny, D.F. (1995) 'IT outsourcing maximises flexibility and control', *Harvard Business Review*, 73(3) (May–June): 84–93.

Lavelle, J.P., Krumwiede, D.W. and Sheu, C. (2000) 'A privatisation model for government outsourcing', *Production and Inventory Management Journal*, 41(2): 45–51.

Leatt, P., Baker, G.R., Halverson, P. and Aird, C. (1997) 'Downsizing, reengineering, and restructuring: long-term implications for healthcare organizations', *Frontiers of Health Services Management*, 13(4): 3–37.

Lee, M. and Stead, V. (1998) 'Human Resource Development in the United Kingdom', *Human Resource Development Quarterly*, 9(3) (Fall): 297–308.

Lee, M.M. (1997) 'Strategic human resource development', *Proceedings of AHRD conference*, Atlanta.

Lei, D. and Slocum, J.W. (1992) 'Global strategy, competence-building and strategic alliances', *California Management Review*, 35(1): 81–97.

Leisman, T. (1999) 'Future sourcing: the next generation of outsourcing opportunities', *Vital Speeches of the Day*, 65(22): 685–90.

Lewis, J.D. (1995) *The Connected Corporation*, Free Press, New York.

Lorenzoni, G. and Baden-Fuller, C. (1995) 'Creating a strategic center to manage a web of partners', *California Management Review*, 37(3): 146–63.

Losey, M. (1998) 'HR comes of age', *HR Magazine*, 43(3): 40–53.

Lundy, K. St (1999) 'Outsourcing savings vanish', *The Australian*, August 17, p. 59.

Macgregor, J., Peterson, S. and Schuftan, C. (1998) 'Downsizing in the Civil Service in developing countries: the golden handshake option revisited', *Public Administrator and Development*, 18(1): 61–76.

Mahe, H. and Perras, C. (1994) 'Successful global strategies for service companies', *Long Range Planning*, 27(1): 36–49.

Marshall, G.E. (2001) 'Back to the future?' *Agency Sales*, 31(2) (February): 37–41.

Mathieson, C. (2001) 'NTL set for IT savings', *The Times*, May 25, p. 17.

McCure, A. (2001) 'IBM signs outsourcing deal with Fiat', *Computing*, May 24, p. 3.

Microsoft.Net (2000) Realising the Next Generation Internet, *http://www.microsoft.com/net/default/ASP[5Feb2001]*

Miles, R.E. and Snow, C. (1994) *Fit, Failure and the Hall of Fame*, The Free Press, New York.

Miles, R.E. and Snow, C.G. (1997) *Organizational Strategy, Structure and Process*, McGraw-Hill, New York.

Mills, D.Q. (1996) 'The changing social contract in American business', *European Management Journal*, 14(5) (October): 451–6.

Mishra, A.K. and Mishra, K.E. (1994) 'The role of mutual trust in effective downsizing strategies', *Human Resource Management*, 33(2): 261–79.

Mishra, K.E, Spreitzer, G. and Mishra, A.K. (1998) 'Preserving employee morale during downsizing', *Sloan Management Review*, 39(2): 83–95.

Mone, M.A. (1994) 'Relationships between self-concepts, aspirations, emotional responses, and intent to leave a downsizing organization', *Human Resource Management*, 33(2): 281–98.

Moran, J. (1999) 'Outsourcing successful if bottom line improves', *Computing Canada*, 25(34): 27–8.

Morrell, N. (1998) 'Outsourcing anxiety', *Telephony*, 235(9): 28–30.

Morrison, D. (1994) 'Psychological contracts and change', *Human Resource Management*, 33(3): 72–84.

Moskal, B. (1993) 'Company loyalty dies: a victim of neglect', *Industry Week*, March, pp. 11–12.

Mullin, R. (1996) 'Managing the outsourced enterprise', *Journal of Business Strategy*, 17(4): 28–32.

Murray, J.Y. and Kotabe, M. (1999) 'Sourcing strategies of US service companies: a modified transaction-cost analysis', *Strategic Management Journal*, 20(9): 791–809.

M2 Communications Ltd. (2001) 'UNISYS', *M2 PRESWIRE*, January 18.

Naden, J. (2000) 'Have a successful APS implementation', *IIE Solutions*, 32(10): 46–57.

Nairn, G. (1999) 'Companies can tap into a growing range of services', *Financial Times, FT-IT Review 3*, August 4, p. 3.

Nairn, G. (1999) 'Vendors seeking long-term strategic partnerships', *Financial Times*, August 4, p. 7.

National Computing Centre (NCC) (1999a) 'Outsourcing reaches desktop', *Press Release*, NCC, June 17, pp. 1–2.

National Computing Centre (NCC) (1999b) *Survey of IT Users 1999*, The National Computing Centre Ltd., Manchester.

Nee, E. (1999) 'Webware for rent', *Fortune*, 140(5): 215–24.

OECD (1997) *Best Practice Guidelines for Contracting Out Government Services*, OECD-PUMA, Paris.

Osborne, D. and Gaebler, T. (1992) *Reinventing Government: How the Entrepreneurial Spirit is Transforming the Public Sector*, Addison-Wesley, Reading.

Outsourcing Government.com (2000) *The Dynamics of Outsourcing in Australia*, pp. 1–4.

Paul, G.L. (2001a) 'The ASP Dilemma', *Electronic Business*, 27(1): 99–102.

Paul, G.L. (2001b) 'Picking a winner', *Network World*, 18(4): 46–9.

Peisch, R. (1995) 'When outsourcing goes awry', *Harvard Business Review*, 73(3) (May–June): 24–30.

Porter, M.E. (1985) *The Competitive Advantage*, The Free Press, New York.

Porter, M.E. (1990) *The Competitive Advantage of Nations*, Macmillan, London.

Prahalad, C. and Hamel, G. (1990) 'The core competence of the corporation', *Harvard Business Review*, 68(3) (May–June): 79–91.

PriceWaterhouseCoopers (1999) *Global Top Decision Makers' Study on Business Process Outsourcing*, PriceWaterhouseCoopers, Yankelovich Partners, Goldstain Consulting Group, New York.

Purcell, J. (1996) 'Contingent workers and human resource strategy: rediscovering the core-periphery dimensions', *Journal of Professional HRM*, No. 5, October, pp. 15–23.

Quinn, J.B. (1999) 'Strategic outsourcing: leveraging knowledge capabilities', *Sloan Management Review*, 40(4) (Summer): 9–22.

Quinn, J.B. and Hilmer, F.G. (1994) 'Strategic outsourcing', *Sloan Management Review*, 35(4) (Summer): 43–55.

Revans, R. (1980) *Action learning: New techniques for management*, Blond and Briggs, London.

Ring, P.S. and Van de Van, A. (1992) 'Structuring cooperative relationships between organizations', *Strategic Management Journal*, 13(3): 438–98.

Rooney, P. (2001) 'Microsoft cements ASP foray', *Computer Reseller News*, Issue 926, January 1, pp. 12–13.

Rothery, B. and Robertson, I. (1995) *The Truth about Outsourcing*, Gower Publishing, Aldershot.

Rousseau, D. (1989) 'Psychological and implied contracts in organizations', *Employee Responsibilities and Rights Journal*, 12(1) (June): 34–78.

Rousseau, D. and Greller, M. (1994) 'Human resource practices: administrative contract makers', *Human Resource Management*, 33(3): 72–81.

Rowley, I. (1999) 'Outsourcing everything', *Institutional Investors*, 33(7): 175–6.

Rumelt, R. (1974) *Strategy, Structure and Economic Performance*, Harvard University Press, Cambridge.

Rysavy, P. (2001) 'E-commerce unleashed', *Network Computing*, 12(2): 56–64.

Savas, E. (1997) *Privatisation: The Key Better Government*, Chatham House, Chatham.

Seurat, R. (1999) 'Sustained and profitable growth', *Business Strategy Review*, 10(1): 53.

Sparrow, P.R. (2000) 'New employee behaviours, work designs and forms of work organization. What is in store for the future of work?', *Journal of Managerial Psychology*, 15(3): 202–18.

Spitzer, A. (1999) 'Steering an academic department through a paradigm shift: the case of a new paradigm for nursing', *Journal of Nursing Education*, 38(7) (October): 312–21.

Standen, P., Daniels, K. and Lamond, D. (1999) 'The home as a workplace: work-family interaction and psychological well-being in telework', *Journal of Occupational Health Psychology*, 4(4).

Sweden, Prime Minister's Office (1994) *Information Technology Wings to Human Ability*, Government Commission on Information Technology, Prime Minister's Office, Stockholm.

Sweezy, P. (1997) 'More (or less) on globalization', *Monthly Review*, 49(4) (September): 1–4.

Szymanski, S. (1996) 'The impact of compulsive competitive tendering on refuse collection services', *Fiscal Studies*, 17(3): 1–19.

Tao, L. (2000) 'Application Service Provider Model: Perspectives and Challenges', paper presented at the International Conference for the Advances in Infrastructure for Electronic Business, Science and Education on the Internet (SSGRR), Aguila, Italy, July 31–August 6.

Taylor, P., Wallage, S. and Chalmers, R. (2001) 'CeBIT2001: ASPs – Is it all just hype?', *Business Week*, March 26, pp. SAS 1-1-4.

Teng, J.T.C., Cheon, M.I. and Grover, V. (1995) 'Decisions to outsource information systems functions: testing a strategy-theoretic discrepancy model', *Decision Sciences*, 26(1): 75–103.

Teresko, J. (1999) 'ERO outsourcing', *Industry Week*, 248(16): 38–41.

The European Council (1994) *Europe and the Global Information Society: Recommendations to the European Council* (Bangemann Report), The European Chancellry, Brussels, May.

Thomas, L.G., III and Waring, G. (1999) 'Competing capitalism: capital investment in America, Germany and Japanese firms', *Strategic Management Journal*, 20(4): 729–48.

Tissen, R., Andriessen, D. and Deprez, L.F. (2000) *The Knowledge Dividend*, Financial Times and Prentice Hall, London.

Torodo, C. (2001) 'IBM pushes hosting', *Computer Reseller News*, Issue 931, February 5, p. 4.

Torodo, C. (2000) 'ASPs Reach Most-Wanted Status', *Computer Reseller News*, February 11, *http:www.ern.com/components/search/Article.asp?*

Torrington, D. and Hall, L. (1998) *Human Resource Management*, Prentice-Hall, London.

Treasury Board of Canada (TBC) (1994) *Blueprint for Renewing Government Service Using Information Technology* (Discussion Draft) Treasury Board of Canada, Ottawa.

Tregaskis, O. (1999) 'Telework in its national context', in K. Daniels, D. Lamond and P. Standen (eds), *Managing Telework*, ITP, London, pp. 97–115.

Tyson, S. and York, A. (2000) *Essentials of HRM*, 4th edn, Butterworth-Heinemann, Oxford.

UK Cabinet Office (1996) *Competing for Quality Policy Review: An Efficiency Unit Scrutiny*, HMSO, London.

US General Accounting Office (1997) *Privatisation: Lessons Learned by State and Local Governments*, GAO-GGD 97-48, Washington.

USA, National Performance Review Office of the Vice President (1993) *Re-engineering Through Information Technology* (Accompanying Report of the National Performance Review Office of the Vice President), Washington DC, September.

USA, State of California (1994) *Task Force on Government Technology Policy and Procurement* (Report to Governor Pete Wilson) State of California, September.

Van Laarhoven, P., Berglund, M., Peters, M., Quelle, G. and Ross, H. (1999) 'Third-party logistics in Europe – five years later', *International Journal of Physical Distribution and Logistic Management – European Supplement* (forthcoming).

Venkatraman, N. and Loh, L. (1994) 'The shifting logic of the IS organization: from technical portfolio to relationship portfolio', *Information Strategy*, 10(2): 5–11.

Vineeta, S. (1994) 'Dancing to the user's tune', *Communications International*, 21(3): 60–65.

Walsh, K. (1991) *Competitive Tendering of Local Authority Services: Initial Experience, Department of the Environment*, HMSO, London.

Walsh, K. (1995) 'Competition and public service delivery' in J. Stewart and G. Stoker (eds), *Local Government in the 1990's*, MacMillan, Basingstoke, pp. 112–32.

Wainewright, P. (2000) 'Anatomy of an ASP: Computing's new genuis', ASP News Review, *http://www.aspnews.com*, January.

West, M. and Patterson, M. (1998) 'Profitable personnel', *People Management*, 4(1): 28–31.

Whalen, M.M. (2000) *World-wide Enterprise ASPForecast and Analysis 1999–2004 – Report W22345*, International Data Corporation (IDC), USA, June.

Willcocks, L. and Fitzgerald, G. (1993) 'Market as opportunity? case studies in outsourcing information technology and services', *Journal of Strategic Information Systems*, 2(3): 223–42.

Willcocks, L. and Fitzgerald, G. (1994) *A Business Guide to IT Outsourcing*, Business Intelligence, London.

Willcocks, L., Fitzgerald, G. and Feeny, D. (1995) 'Outsourcing IT: the strategic implications', *Long Range Planning*, 28(5): 59–70.

Williamson, O.E. (1988) 'The logic of economic organization', *Journal of Law Economics and Organization*, 4(1): 65–93.

Williamson, O.E. (1996) 'Economic and organizations: a primer', *California Management Review*, 38(2): 131–46.

Willman, J. (1999) 'Unilever to focus on core "power brands"', *Financial Times*, September 22, p. 25.

Index